Additional Praise for the Topgrading System

"At American Power Conversion (APC), Topgrading has dramatically increased our success rate hiring A players. Our commitment to the Topgrading process is higher than ever!"

—Andrew Cole, senior vice president, human resources

"I've had firsthand experience with Brad, and his approach to finding talent and fitting the talent to the job's requirements works. Brad's books demystify the concept of Topgrading, and as he draws from thousands of real experiences, he provides a road map for building successful management teams. I wish he'd put this on paper a long time ago."

—Joseph C. Lawler, president and CEO, CMGI

"When I look back at the dramatic success of our company, I can clearly point to the implementation of Topgrading as the pivotal moment that made our success possible. I implore every business owner to make Topgrading mandatory in their company. A Topgraded team is the ultimate secret weapon to crush the competition."

—Richard Rossi, cochairman, EnvisionEMI

"Brad Smart's Topgrading principles are a must-read for anyone interested in winning! Our executives and customers rave about how the Topgrading interview tools and processes consistently swing the odds in favor of selecting only A Players . . . resulting in innovation, incremental revenue, and increased operating income throughout the enterprise."

—John H. Dickey, senior vice president,
Hillenbrand Industries, Inc. and Hill-Rom Company

"I found *Topgrading* to be highly compelling, specifically in its approach to interviewing candidates and increasing the effectiveness of my hiring decisions. The Topgrading workshop introduced a comprehensive set of tools—much more revealing than approaches I've used in the past. Highly recommended for any manager looking to sharpen their ability to identify the 'right' candidate for the job."

—Fred Harding, vice president, Global Alliances, Taleo

"Have you ever hired someone for whom you had high expectations only to suffer bitter disappointment in that individual's performance? Have you ever paid the heavy price of search, hire, and relocate, only to witness internal disruption as the person failed in his job? Have you ever chosen the wrong man or woman to advance to more responsibility? Dr. Brad Smart's groundbreaking research shows that most hiring decisions are mistakes. Winning companies have learned to Topgrade—they succeed at getting and promoting the best. You can too. Dr. Smart tells you how."

—Curt Clawson, president, CEO, and
chairman, Hayes Lemmerz, International

"Sales turnover is the single biggest and costliest challenge we have in our company. This book gives the reader a *practical* way to quantify all parts to the sourcing and hiring process. Most especially it assists in eliminating *emotional* mistakes in the interviewing process. Worth the read and then using it."

—John King, chief executive officer, Quench USA

"In the fight against cardiovascular disease and stroke Topgrading has helped us raise an additional $50 million over the preceding year."

—Cass Wheeler, CEO, American Heart Association

"The book *Topgrading* is the single most important and relevant business book that I have ever read."

—Jon A. Boscia, chairman and CEO (retired),
Lincoln National Corporation

"Topgrading is a proven strategy for hiring A Players and building dream teams. Companies and individuals who Topgrade gain a talent advantage—they consistently outperform the competition and reap the rewards of excellence."

> —Robert H. Bohannon, chairman, president,
> and CEO, Viad Corp.

"Topgrading is a philosophy and practice that clearly distinguishes organizations that desire to reach and maintain world-class status. Brad Smart's selection process is built on technically correct assessment techniques, and validated through years of successful experiences with a wide variety of positions and organizations. It works!"

> —Mel McCall, senior vice president,
> human resources, CompUSA

"Topgrading is not just desirable but essential for organization success in this competitive world. Brad has helped me grow, and has helped DSC evolve from a warehousing company to a growth-oriented, leading-edge supply-chain management company."

> —Ann Drake, CEO, DSC Logistics

"I have used Brad for over ten years in my ongoing efforts to build and enhance our own A team. Topgrading represents the kind of breakthrough I would expect from Dr. Smart. I will use it as standard practice here at DCM. American industry, I believe, will adopt Topgrading as a necessary human resource optimization process in order to be competitive and survive on a global basis."

> —David Gottstein, president, Dynamic Capital Management

"The most useful and professional book I have ever read on the selection interview. It represents a true burst of quality. Smart's writing style is fast-paced, personal, and engaging. He writes as an astute observer of human behavior."

> —Dr. Paul M. Muchinsky, *Personnel Psychology*

Topgrading

for Sales

Also by Bradford D. Smart

*Topgrading: How Leading Companies Win by
Hiring, Coaching, and Keeping the Best People*

*The Smart Interviewer: Tools and Techniques
for Hiring the Best*

*Smart Parenting: How to Raise Happy,
Can-Do Kids* (with Kate Smart Mursau, Psy.D.)

Also by Greg Alexander

*Making the Number: How to Use Sales
Benchmarking to Drive Performance*

for Sales

WORLD-CLASS METHODS TO INTERVIEW, HIRE, AND COACH TOP SALES REPRESENTATIVES

Bradford D. Smart, Ph.D., and Greg Alexander

PORTFOLIO

PORTFOLIO
Published by the Penguin Group
Penguin Group (USA) Inc., 375 Hudson Street,
New York, New York 10014, U.S.A.
Penguin Group (Canada), 90 Eglinton Avenue East, Suite 700,
Toronto, Ontario, Canada M4P 2Y3
(a division of Pearson Penguin Canada Inc.)
Penguin Books Ltd, 80 Strand, London WC2R 0RL, England
Penguin Ireland, 25 St. Stephen's Green, Dublin 2, Ireland
(a division of Penguin Books Ltd)
Penguin Books Australia Ltd, 250 Camberwell Road, Camberwell,
Victoria 3124, Australia
(a division of Pearson Australia Group Pty Ltd)
Penguin Books India Pvt Ltd, 11 Community Centre, Panchsheel Park,
New Delhi – 110 017, India
Penguin Group (NZ), 67 Apollo Drive, Rosedale, North Shore 0632,
New Zealand (a division of Pearson New Zealand Ltd)
Penguin Books (South Africa) (Pty) Ltd, 24 Sturdee Avenue,
Rosebank, Johannesburg 2196, South Africa

Penguin Books Ltd, Registered Offices:
80 Strand, London WC2R 0RL, England

First published in 2008 by Portfolio,
a member of Penguin Group (USA) Inc.

10 9 8 7 6 5 4 3 2 1

LIBRARY OF CONGRESS CATALOGING IN PUBLICATION DATA
Smart, Bradford D., 1944–
   Topgrading for sales : world-class methods to interview, hire, and coach top sales
representatives / Brad Smart and Greg Alexander.
      p. cm.
   Includes index.
   ISBN 978-1-59184-206-4
   1. Sales management.   2. Selling.   I. Alexander, Greg, 1970–   II. Title.
   HF5438.4.S536 2008
   658.3'11—dc22

                                                          2007040380

Printed in the United States of America
Set in Minion and Berthold Akzidenz Grotesk

To the hundreds of A player sales managers who have embraced Topgrading methods, doubling and even tripling the high performers on their sales team.

BRAD SMART

To the sales leaders who have embraced Sales Benchmark Index's disruption of the sales improvement industry. Their commitment to Peer Produced Best Practices is raising the collective capabilities of the global sales force.

GREG ALEXANDER

Contents

for Sales

Introduction

You can double the number of high performers on your sales team. Really! The next few paragraphs should convince you of this, or don't bother reading this book. You'd rather spend your time creating sales opportunities than reading books, right? However, this book may be the most important read of your career. Sales managers who read and apply the very straightforward Topgrading methods have dramatically improved their hiring success.

Such improvements require your doing more than just skimming this book. Excellent sales rep hiring is a chain with many links, and chances are, your hiring chain has plenty of rusty or missing links. We present the very best practices in a simple, practical way. Here are those 10 links:

The 10 Links in the Hiring Chain

1. Construct a Topgrading Scorecard for Sales Representatives, to identify *all* the crucial accountabilities and competencies (see page 55).
2. Analyze your sales team, using the Annual Talent Review Form, to nail down who are your keepers . . . and who are not. Nudge out the nots (see page 14).
3. Analyze your past mis-hires, using the Cost of Mis-Hires Form for Sales Representatives, to fully understand how expensive it is *not* to Topgrade (see page 16).
4. Develop your Virtual Bench, your list of prospects to call, so that you rarely have to resort to running ads or paying recruiters (see page 25).

5. Use the Topgrading Career History Form and Sales Representative Telephone Screen questions to save about 10 hours each time you hire a sales rep (see pages 58 and 31).

6. Use round-robin competency (behavioral) interviews to screen finalist candidates (see page 75).

7. Conduct a Topgrading Interview in order to gain the deepest insights into your finalists, for *all* crucial competencies (see page 62).

8. Ask finalist candidates to arrange personal reference calls with bosses they've had in the past decade, both to get reference opinions *and* to motivate candidates to be honest in interviews (see page 93).

9. Coach your sales reps regularly. Ask each to create an Individual Development Plan, and follow up on it quarterly to ensure that your reps will perform at their peak.

10. Subscribe to the free monthly Topgrading newsletter, *Topgrading Tips,* at www.SmartTopgrading.com, for regular tips on how to create a top sales team (see page 52). And subscribe to receive the free quarterly Sales Benchmark Index (SBI) World Class 100 Report at www.SalesBenchmarkIndex.com for insights into hiring trends being adopted by the world's top performing sales organizations (see page 53).

Hundreds of sales managers have learned the single most valuable link in the chain, the most revealing interview method ever devised—the Topgrading Interview. Every sales manager we have heard of who achieved 90 percent high performers on their sales team used the Topgrading Interview. And this silver-bullet interview technique—Brad Smart's thorough, chronological interview—is amazingly simple to understand. Master those questions, and you are well under way to increasing the number of high performers on your sales team.

The Topgrading Interview has been praised and embraced by top business leaders, many of whom attribute much of the success of their company to this method. Picking the right people is *that* important to CEOs. It's that important to every VP Sales, too. Your bonus, performance rating, and promotability all will be enhanced when you pick better people—not just 60 percent who make quota but 80 percent and even 90 percent who far exceed quota.

Greg Alexander is sure you can do it, because he did it. He learned Brad's interview method, used it, and in one year took the 12th (out of 14) region of tech giant EMC to the number-one position. It was a tough time. A recession was beginning, EMC laid off seven thousand employees, and Greg's team was cut from 199 to 177. Only 41 percent of his sales team made quota the year before he took over, and of the 36 sales reps hired the year before, only 29 percent made quota.

Greg Topgraded. Underperformers were coached and trained, and they either made quota (a stretch goal, well above industry standard) or they left. Using Topgrading hiring methods, Greg hired 36 new reps, and only one year later, 95 percent of them were already achieving industry-average quota. That's Topgrading—from 27 percent making quota to 95 percent, in one year! Furthermore, after just one year, 87 percent were achieving Greg's stretch goal, 160 percent of industry standard.

Greg's new A team actually increased revenue during the recession, and theirs was the only region to do so. Furthermore, the new A players made the region number one in landing new customers and in sales of new products. As Greg put it at the time, "The results were

> *That's Togpgrading—from 27 percent making quota to 95 percent, in one year!*

described throughout the company as amazing, but it should never be amazing when top sales people produce great results. A can-do attitude, drive, and resourcefulness enable A players to grab successes out of the jaws of defeat, while mediocre sales reps blame the recession or something else for their mediocre results."

Here's our promise to you: Use the methods and tools provided in this book, and you should easily double the percentage of high performing sales reps. Chapter 6 explains additional methods and tools to take you to 80 or 90 percent high performers, just as Greg did. But hey! Let's get started, learn the basics, and immediately start hiring better.

CHAPTER 1

The Joys of Having A Player Sales Reps

This chapter will give you just enough theory to understand what you need to know to successfully apply the Topgrading methods provided in the subsequent chapters. We'll give you some statistics that show how widespread sales rep failure is and what the consequences are (hint—all bad!). A sophisticated model for success, developed by Sales Benchmark Index, will be introduced, and case studies will show how brilliantly the model works—for sales managers, for their successful sales reps, and for the shareholders. This entire chapter is intended to get and hold your attention so that you can't help diving into and totally absorbing the practical methods presented in the rest of the book.

Hiring high performing sales reps is difficult for most sales managers. Duh—you didn't need us to give you that epiphany! Hiring is tough because companies don't let managers give out references, so candidates hype positives and conceal negatives, confident they will get away with it. Go into any bookstore and try to find a book on job hunting that encourages real honesty. There is no such book! Job hunting manuals teach job hunters to fake their resumes and con their way through those short competency interviews. All of these dynamics put you, the sales manager, at a disadvantage.

It gets even worse. Your sales candidates are experienced at selling, and the product they are selling in the interview is themselves, so their product knowledge is better than yours. They understand buyers like you, because they've worked for sales managers. They know the sales manager's motivations and needs, and they try to manipulate the interview to hit his or her hot buttons. Sales managers are frequently . . . well . . . desperate. If their territory is growing or they are replacing an underperformer, they are eager to get someone on board. A delay will cost them money; they are paid on sales, and an open job generates zero sales. It's understandable if corners are cut. Although sales managers rationally know a poor hire can be costly, having no rep in a territory is also costly. "Bad breath is better than no breath," as they say.

Sales Benchmark Index research reveals that between 1996 and 2006, the failure rate for sales reps nationally was about 40 percent. To be specific, 40 percent failed to achieve their stated annual sales goals. According to an *Inc.* magazine survey, the job category with the most terminations is sales rep. Not coincidentally, turnover among sales reps during the same time period was . . . 40 percent! Turnover is defined as percentage of sales reps leaving a job in a 12-month period for any reason, and it includes a few percentage points for good reasons, like getting promoted. Poor hiring decisions lead to poor results and to replacement of sales managers. The average tenure for a sales manager is only 19 months.

According to the federal government, there are 20 million sales reps in the United States. With a 40-percent turnover rate, eight million sales reps change jobs each year. Sales Benchmark Index and Smart & Associates estimate the average cost of a mis-hire to be about $600,000 for a sales rep with a $100,000 base compensation. In

> *The average cost of a mis-hire is about $600,000 for a sales rep with a $100,000 base compensation.*

a subsequent chapter, we'll give you a useful tool for calculating the costs of *your* mis-hires, but for now let's just work with the research.

According to A player sales managers, only 25 percent of the 20 million sales reps are A players. With a lower standard, 40 percent miss quota annually. So, depending on the standard, between eight million and 15 million are mis-hires. Whether your sales reps are telemarketers or million-dollar producers, your mis-hires cost your company a fortune and cost you peace of mind and bonus dollars.

Definitions: A Player and Topgrading

Before spelling out methods to help you hire sales reps better, let's get on the same page with terminology.

Just because someone hasn't been fired doesn't exactly qualify that someone as an A player. In our experience, the "80–20 Rule" fits many sales organizations—20 percent of the sales reps achieve 80 percent of the sales.

We define *A player* as "best of breed"—a sales rep in the top 10 percent of those available, whatever the base salary and bonus arrangement might be. These are your high performers. A players exceed industry standard by 150 percent in many industries. To us, and maybe you, the sales reps who barely achieve industry standard are the B players—reps between the 10th and 35th percentile available for the pay. Over the years, A player sales managers have said that before Topgrading they had only 25 percent A players, 35 percent B players, and 40 percent C players. But Topgraders achieve 80 and even 90 percent high performers, A players.

While we're giving definitions, let's define Topgrading: It means packing your sales team with all high performing A players. Topgrading is explained in Brad Smart's best-selling book, *Topgrading: How Companies Win by Hiring, Coaching, and Keeping the Best People* (Portfolio, New York, 2005). This bible of Topgrading presents case studies in which companies were much more successful because they embraced the Topgrading methods. The typical company started with only 25 percent of people hired or promoted turning out to be A players. The book has dozens of case studies in which companies improved to 80 and even 90 percent A players hired. Many are leading organizations and companies, like General Electric, the American Heart Association, Hillenbrand, Honeywell, Lincoln Financial, and many others. Their managers learned to pick people better; you will too!

One example is Kennametal, a $2.5 billion supplier of tooling, engineered components, and advanced materials used in production processes. Kennametal launched Topgrading in 2003, managers participated in workshops, and Kevin Walling, vice president and chief human resources officer, said, "We have used the concepts of Topgrading for years . . . which has resulted in significantly greater success in hiring the *right* person for the job."

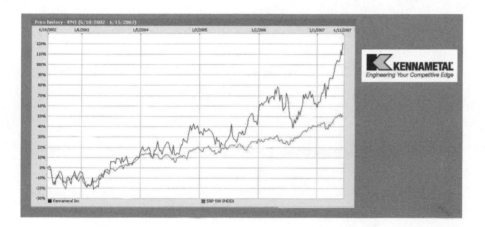

A Player Sales Reps—Let's Count the Joys!

The joys of having high performing sales reps are many, because A players:

1. "get" the strategy that Chief Sales Officers create and make it reality;
2. assure that your monthly, quarterly, and annual forecasts are met;
3. assure high R&D yield. Marketing originates ideas, Engineering develops them, but only the A players convince prospects to buy them;
4. innovate. A players are the first to sense market trends, and they are your and Marketing's early-alert system;
5. provide you bench strength for promotability to Sales Manager;
6. sell at higher prices than other reps can sell;

7. are talent magnets. They attract other A players you can hire;
8. extend customer life, which you know is money in the bank;
9. lessen the need for managerial overhead. You can supervise 15 A players, but only half a dozen B and C players, because lower performers are higher maintenance;
10. enable organizational harmony. Marketing, Engineering, and Production all love to blame your sales team for their own problems, while A player sales teams make everyone look good.

OK, you knew all of this. You *want* to hire better. But are Topgrading methods much better than what you've been using?

The 30-to-1 Topgrading Advantage

Please bear with us and do a little exercise that will explain why you, when you are a Topgrader, will have a *huge* advantage in hiring sales reps.

Here's the exercise: Suppose you inherited 100 sales reps, and 10 are terrible. After giving them a chance to succeed, you conclude that these 10 are hopeless, and you *need* to have 10 high performers, A players, in those jobs. It doesn't matter whether the C players are trying to sell $15 million homes or they are telemarketers.

Question: How many sales reps do you have to hire, and how many do you then have to fire, in order to end up with 10 A players?

Well, if your success rate is the typical 25 percent, you have to hire 40, fire your 30 mis-hires, fire the 10 mis-hires you inherited, and . . . finally you have your 10 A players. What a bloody mess! No sales organization could survive such turmoil.

> The non-Topgrader has 30 mis-hires to the Topgrader's 1 mis-hire; hence, the "30-to-1 Topgrading advantage."

Aah, but the Topgraders who enjoy 90-percent success only have to hire 11 sales reps and fire 1 to end up with 10 A players. That's doable, isn't it! The non-Topgrader has 30 mis-hires to the Topgrader's 1 mis-hire; hence, the "30-to-1 Topgrading advantage."

This was so much fun, do you want to do it again, lowering the bar? Since 60 percent of sales reps achieve their targets annually, let's make the assumption that the mis-hire rate is 40 percent, not 75 percent. You have a 60-percent success rate in hiring, and you want to replace all poor performers with, not high performers, just adequate performers who make their industry average quota. OK, then you have to hire 17 and fire 7 to end up with 10 B players. So there is still a 7-to-1 Topgrading advantage, even if you replace C players with B players and not A players.

The Sales Benchmark Index Formula for Sales Success

Greg used his years with EMC and other companies to refine a very practical model for sales managers to measure the most important things and fix what's not working. The formula is:

Sales has too long been an art. It is perhaps the last bastion of aimless gut-feel decision making in the business world. Operational excellence, Six Sigma, lean manufacturing, the Toyota method, and reengineering are all benchmarking methods that are used to identify the right metrics, gather the metrics, analyze the findings, and address what needs fixing. Yet they are all typically applied to other disciplines in the corporation—finance, marketing, distribution, even information technology. Sales, however, has escaped this type of scrutiny. As a result, sales managers too often wing it, and winging it rarely succeeds. Indeed, it's no coincidence that there is a 40 percent turnover rate in sales jobs and that 40 percent of sales reps fail to meet annual quota.

The Sales Benchmark Index Formula for Sales Success enables the sales leader to break down the process of acquiring and retaining customers into its essential elements. The five components in the formula can all be measured and benchmarked against industry averages and world class performance.

The Sales Benchmark Index at Work

Here's an example, one chosen because the talent levels before and after Topgrading are so typical.

Activities	1 call per day
Conversions	10 percent
Transactions	$50K per deal
Talent	50 sales reps (38 percent missing quota)
Time	240 sales days

The annual sales for a division of ABCD Technology is $60M:

$$\text{Activities} \times \text{Conversions} \times \text{Transactions} \times \text{Talent} \times \text{Time} = \$60M$$

The CEO asked the VP Sales for a 20-percent increase, to $72M. The VP Sales initially attempted to increase all the components by 20 percent. His plan was:

$$\text{1.2 Calls/Day} \times \text{12\% Closure} \times \$60,000\text{ Average Deal} \times \text{60 Sales Reps} \times \text{240 Days Per Year}$$
$$= \$124.4\text{ Million Annual Sales}$$

Was it realistic to project sales increases from $60M to double that amount? No way. What in fact happened was:

$$\text{1.2 Calls/Day} \times \text{7\% Closure} \times \$55,000\text{ Average Deal} \times \text{60 Sales Reps} \times \text{240 Days Per Year}$$
$$= \$66.5\text{ Million Annual Sales}$$

In real life, all the variables interact with each other. Talent and the marketplace affect what can actually happen. In this case, the marketplace would not accept $60K deals, and so transaction size increased from $50K to $55K but not to the projected $60K. The VP Sales hired 10 more reps, but each was a little less productive: Their conversion rate declined. The huge fly in the ointment was hiring that produced 38 percent underperforming sales reps—23 of the 60 failed to achieve their annual objective.

But then the VP Sales discovered Topgrading, and a year later 85 percent of the reps hit target. By increasing the number of successful sales reps from 37 to 51, the conversion rate shot up to 10 percent, enabling sales to increase 50 percent, to $95M!

The Sales Benchmark Index Formula for Sales Success showed the VP Sales that the *quality* of the sales force would have to be improved to attain the CEO's objectives. As it became clear that the $72M goal would be exceeded, and in fact was exceeded by $23M, the VP Sales was quite the hero. And the hero became richer, because of a mega bonus earned!

As the Sales Benchmark Index Formula for Sales Success shows, the single most powerful factor in improving any sales organization is talent, and Topgrading is the way to find it.

CHAPTER 2

Analyze Your Sales Team

First things first. Before you analyze your sales team, you need to figure out exactly what you want in a sales rep. It's time to write a job description, right? *Yawn!* Those documents are usually boilerplate—worthless.

Create a Sales Rep Scorecard

A better method is to create a Job Scorecard, a document that spells out exactly what the *accountabilities* are. To create your Sales Rep Scorecard:

- Identify the CEO's strategy and mission.

- Identify specific accountabilities based on the most important metrics.

- Identify additional mission-critical competencies.

Your Sales Rep Scorecard assures that *all* competencies you want to scrutinize in interviews (quotas, sales approaches, motivation, resourcefulness, etc.) will be clear. Appendix A, the Topgrading Scorecard for Sales Representatives, is an example. Please take a look at it now. It happens to include 33 competencies. Yours might include 15 or 50.

Why spend the time writing a Sales Rep Scorecard? We've assessed and coached hundreds of sales managers, and those who did not nail down all the crucial accountabilities regretted it. If there are no accountabilities for margins, your sales people will sell unprofitably.

You know this, yet busy sales managers sometimes nail down some, but not all, of the goals they want achieved.

An entrepreneur was involved in the creation of a Job Scorecard for a prospective VP Sales position for one of his portfolio companies. This company manufactures products sold mostly to mom-and-pop retailers. The questioning led the CEO to exclaim, "My God, our sales force should be targeting the big-box stores like Wal-Mart, not tiny retailers! We need a new, upgraded sales force!" Writing Job Scorecards is a discipline that can refine strategy.

As you compose the scorecard, consider *all* numbers you hold people accountable for—revenues, margins, sale of new products, customer retention, landing new customers, etc. And don't include just sales metrics, but consider additional competencies you value—how much of a team player the person is, whether the person is apt to remain with you, whether the person is diligent in completing sales bookwork, whether the person might have management potential, etc. Some of the most impressive Topgrading has taken place when the sales manager fired a number-one producer who was totally disruptive, causing other sales reps to produce less. If teamwork is *that* important, include it as a competency in the job scorecard, so that your interviews will focus on it.

The single most important competency in this example of a Job Scorecard is the last—resourcefulness. Resourcefulness is a combination of motivation (number 24) and judgment (number 28). Resourceful sales reps figure out how to get over, around, or through barriers to success. The most resourceful reps are almost always those with the best track record (number 1).

Conduct an Annual Talent Review

With your Sales Rep Scorecard created, it's time to analyze your sales team. Use the Talent Review Form for a quick, revealing ranking of all your sales reps.

 **Talent Review**

Name	
Company/Department	
Date	

Rank Order	A Players	Comments

Rank Order	B Players	Comments

Rank Order	C Players	Comments

% A Players = ____%   (A player: top 10% of talent available for the pay)

% B Players = ____%   (B player: next 25%)

% C Players = ____%   (C player: below top 35%)

Keeping your newly created scorecard in mind, simply rank order your entire sales team from the top performer to the lowest performer, and put them into the A, B, and C categories based on whether you think they are in the top 10 percent of talent available for the pay (A player), the next 25 percent (B player), or below the top 35 percent (C player).

If that standard seems too high for you right now, then just rank sales reps top to bottom, and use two categories: Achieves Industry Standard and Below Industry Standard. If you do not know the Industry Standard, visit www.SalesBenchmarkIndex.com to get access to a database of close to 11,000 companies across 19 industries.

OK, now you have your rank order. Think about keeping your arms around your most valued sales reps, and look carefully at your costly mis-hires. Should you replace them?

Calculate the Cost of Mis-Hires

This is one of the most illuminating exercises you'll ever do, and it only takes about 15 minutes for each mis-hire. Do it for *all* your mis-hires, so you can calculate a grand total. It won't be "grand," because staring at the cost of mis-hire numbers will drive home what it really costs *not* to Topgrade. We've made it somewhat easy—just use the Cost of Mis-Hires Form for Sales Representatives:

Cost of Mis-Hires Form
for Sales Representatives

Job title of person mis-hired or mispromoted: _____

Dates person was in position: from _____ until _____.

    (If person was successful in previous job but failed in a new job, calculate costs only for the years the person was in the new job.)

Reason for leaving:

Quit ___, Fired (or forced to resign) ___, Transferred ___, Demoted ___, Retired ___, Died ___, Other ___.

1. **Total costs in hiring the person** $_____
   - Recruitment/search fees (any guarantee? if so, was money recovered?)
   - Outside testing, interviewing, record checking, physical exam
   - HR department time and administrative costs (for all candidates)
   - Travel costs (for all candidates, spouses, other executives traveling to meet candidate)
   - Time/expenses of non-HR people (all candidates)
   - Relocation (moving household goods, purchasing house for candidate)

2. **Compensation:** (sum for all years person was in job) $_____
   - Base ($_____ x number of years)
   - Bonuses (signing, performance, etc.) for all years
   - Stock options (realized for all years), benefits (insurance, 401k, etc.), car, clubs
   - Other forms of compensation

3. **Maintaining person in job:** (sum for all years person was in job) $_____
   - Administrative assistant for all years
   - Office rental (incl. electricity, etc.) for all years
   - Furniture, computer, equipment, travel for all years
   - Training
   - Other "maintaining" costs

4. **Total severance:** $_____
   - Severance fee (salary, benefits, use of office), lawyer fees
   - Outplacement counseling fee
   - Costs in lawsuits caused by the person (EEOC, harassment, EPA, OSHA, etc.)
   - Administrative costs in separation, wasted time of people in separation
   - Bad press (loss of corporate goodwill, reputation)

5. **Mistakes/Failures, missed and wasted business opportunities:** $_____
   (For example… drove a key customer away, impaired customer loyalty, failed to enter new hot market, embezzled $1M, launched three "dog" products)

6. **Disruption:** $_____
   (Costs of inefficiency in the organization, lower morale, lower productivity, impaired teamwork)

7. **Other:** $_____

8. **Sum Of All Costs (#1–#7)** $_____

Enter conservative estimates of costs in all the categories—don't inflate anything. Just look at each category and the components in it, and add up all the components in each category. Ugh! The cost of mis-hires is painfully high, isn't it?

We've done enough of these analyses to offer a fairly typical composite example, one in which the base salary was $100,000 and the sales rep lasted one year:

Hiring Costs—$23,000. The assumptions are $15,000 (recruiter fee of 15 percent of base salary), $100 (background check), $750 (travel), and the rest in time wasted by you, Human Resources (HR), and others.

Compensation—$151,000. The assumptions are $100,000 (base salary for one year), $10,000 (signing bonus), $10,000 (stock options), $25,000 (benefits load), $6,000 (auto expense). No bonus, since targets were not met.

Maintenance—$14,000. The assumptions are $12,000 (one trip per month @ $1,000) and $2,000 (annual training allowance).

Severance—$25,000. The assumption is three-month severance.

Opportunity Costs—$250,000. The assumptions are that the annual revenue quota was $500,000 and that the rep achieved $250,000.

Disruption Costs—$100,000. The assumptions are that there was a customer the rep lost and that the annual revenues from the customer were $100,000.

Assumptions	Amount	Percentage
Hiring costs	$23,000	4%
Compensation	$151,000	27%
Maintenance	$14,000	2%
Severance	$25,000	4%
Opportunity Costs	$250,000	45%
Disruption costs	$100,000	18%
Total	*$563,000*	*100%*

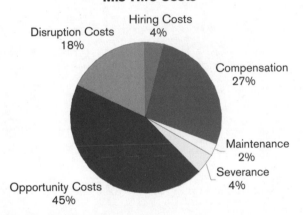

Mis-Hire Costs

These two exercises, the rankings and the costs of all the mis-hires currently on your team, give you a solid analysis of your sales team. Add just one more part of the analysis: Think of the impact your mis-hires have had on your work life. Ouch! In Topgrading workshops, we've begun asking how many hours per year are wasted on each mis-hire: It's hundreds! Most sales managers figure that 90 percent of the frustrations, excessively long work weeks, and disappointments in the job come from those mis-hires.

The total mis-hire cost of almost $600,000 for a sales rep earning a base comp of $100,000 is just an average. You might consider the assumptions too high or too low, so we encourage you to do your own estimates, using the Cost of Mis-Hires Form for Sales Representatives. Perhaps your sales force averages only $25,000 base and $5,000 bonus—no problem! Do the estimates for your last few mis-hires, and see what reality is in your business. The costs, though far less than $500,000, will still be shockingly high, and the analysis will motivate you to improve your hiring success.

Financial Benefits of Topgrading

Let's do a couple more analyses—the sorts a CFO and CEO want. The first analysis is simple, showing how much money a company saves, just in terms of cutting the costs of mis-hires. It's a net-present-value (NPV) analysis.

How to Save $96 Million in Costs of Mis-Hires

Consider a 400-person sales force that is average in both annual turnover (40 percent) and mis-hire rate (40 percent). The total cost to the business over a five year period is summarized in the following table:

FORTY-PERCENT MIS-HIRE RATE						
Year	1	2	3	4	5	Total
Total Sales People	400	400	400	400	400	
Annual Turnover Rate	40%	40%	40%	40%	40%	
Total Hires	160	160	160	160	160	800
Mis-Hire Percentage	40%	40%	40%	40%	40%	
Total Mis-Hires	64	64	64	64	64	320
Annual Cost ($K)	$36,064	$36,064	$36,064	$36,064	$36,064	$180,320
Discounted Annual Cost ($K)	$30,053	$25,044	$20,870	$17,392	$14,493	$107,853
Net Present Value ($K) $(107,853)						

With a \$563K cost per mis-hire, hiring mistakes in the sales department over the next five years represent a \$180M problem. Applying a 20 percent discount rate, which in CFO-speak is also known as the cost of capital and is used to convert future dollars into present values, the hiring woes will cost the company \$108M according to NPV calculations.

Let's assume that after reading this book, the CEO realizes the company is underperforming its peers in terms of hiring success and decides to deploy Topgrading according to the plan provided. The organization sets a conservative first year goal of reducing its turnover and mis-hire rates from 40 percent to 20 percent. Appendix E presents the full analysis, but the bottom line is this: In the first year alone, the company saves over \$22M, yet the cost of rolling out Topgrading is only a very small fraction of this amount.

Impressed with the early results from year one, the company decides to further embrace Topgrading in year two and sets the goal of achieving world-class status by reducing its turnover and mis-hire rate to 10 percent. The \$180M problem is reduced by 90 percent to \$18M in real dollars, or from \$108M to \$12M in today's dollars. This tells us that Topgrading can reduce the 40 percent mis-hire problem to 20 percent in year one, followed by a reduction to 10 percent in years two through five. It also tells us that Topgrading can save the company \$96M over five years, according to NPV calculations.

How to Increase Your Market Cap \$75 Million

At this point, we have shown that the total cost associated with mis-hiring sales people is staggering. But it would be doing the business case a disservice to stop here. Organizations and their leadership teams must answer to shareholders, who care most about share-price appreciation. They do not value day-to-day cost-cutting measures that don't produce a return for them.

So can Topgrading really generate the results shareholders are asking for? Let's just say that if you were impressed with the cost computations, you will be blown away by how Topgrading boosts share price. (By the way, have you been granted stock options?) This is a more complex analysis, and a thorough explanation is provided in Appendix E, but here are the key points:

The P/E (price/earnings) ratio of the technology sector is currently at 22. This means that the average stock trading for $22 per share has a per share earnings of $1. In the above example, if a technology company increased earnings 50 percent, from $1.00 to $1.50, and the P/E ratio remained at 22, the stock price would surge to $33! (By the way, how many stock options does your CEO have?) And Topgrading will increase a $220M market capitalization to $330M. The result from the increase in earnings is an additional $110M in shareholder wealth, or a 50-percent return on shareholder investment.

Let's look next at a detailed case study to see how Topgrading and the sales talent lever of the SBI Formula for Sales Success drives mammoth shareholder value creation. Here are the base financial assumptions for a technology company with 400 sales people.*

Income Statement	Amount ($)	% of Revenue
Revenue	$200M	100%
Cost of Revenue	$92M	46%
Operating Expenses	$94M	47%
SG&A	$70M	35%
Cost of Sales	$40M	20%
G&A Expense	$30M	15%
R&D	$24M	12%
Other Expenses	$4M	2%
Earnings	$10M	5%

Shares Outstanding	10,000,000
Share Price	$22
Earnings Per Share (EPS)	$1
P/E Ratio	22
Market Cap	$220M

* The source of the financial-ratio data is the 541 companies in the information technology sector whose revenues are greater than $100M, based on 2006 financial performance according to Yahoo! Finance.

Based on the mis-hire cost computations above, deploying Topgrading to reduce the mis-hire rate from 40 percent to 20 percent in the first year of the project reduces the size of the problem from $36M to $9M in year one. Of this $27M reduction, roughly $17M goes toward revenue growth and $10M toward gross Cost of Sales reductions. Accounting for increased costs associated

> That's right, $44M in shareholder value was created simply by leveraging Topgrading in the first year of deployment!

with the additional revenue creation, the Cost of Sales as a percentage of revenue shrinks from 20 percent to 19.5 percent. The company's profitability increases from 5 percent to 5.5 percent, a 10-percent improvement. With 10M shares outstanding, the new EPS is $1.20. Assuming the P/E multiple remains constant at 22, the new share price is $26.40, up from $22. The impact on the market cap is a staggering $44M increase, from $220M to $264M. That's right, $44M in shareholder value was created simply by leveraging Topgrading in the first year of deployment!

Blown away with the first year success of Topgrading, the leadership team decides this project will not suffer the fate of many other corporate initiatives and be phased out after the first few months. Instead, they further embrace Topgrading and set a more aggressive world-class goal of less than 10-percent turnover and greater than 90-percent hiring success for year two. The company's profitability increases from 5.5 percent to 6 percent, a 9 percent improvement. With 10M shares outstanding, the new EPS is $1.34. Assuming the P/E multiple remains constant at 22, the new share price is $29.50, up 12 percent from $26.40. The impact on the market cap is even more impressive, as it surges from $264M to $295M. Yes, another $31M in shareholder value was created in the second year of deployment simply by leveraging Topgrading to improve the hiring practices of the organization!

What an opportunity! Topgrading your 400-person sales force would have to produce a 20-percent shareholder return while creating more than $44M in market cap value in the first 12 months of deployment, followed by a 12-percent return and another $31M market cap increase during the second 12 months!

Before moving on, the results in this example are worth repeating. *Through the P/E leverage, Topgrading produces a 20-percent shareholder revenue increase, generating over $44M in shareholder wealth in the first year, and a total of 34-percent shareholder return—16-percent compound annual growth rate (CAGR)—creating $75M in shareholder wealth, in the first two years of deployment.*

This is simply too large an opportunity to ignore. So, let's cut mis-hires to the absolute minimum, starting with the best way to recruit high producers.

CHAPTER 3

The Best Sales Rep Recruiting Methods

You've created a Topgrading Job Scorecard, performed a Talent Review of your team, calculated the costs of mis-hiring sales reps, and learned both the costs of mis-hires to the company as a whole and how Topgrading sales can turboboost stock price. So you are well on your way to hiring better. It's time to take a hard look at your recruitment methods, because in the next few paragraphs you'll learn methods that will get more of the right prospects into your pipeline of talent and save you 20 hours or more for each rep hired.

This chapter will teach you three more of the crucial links in the sales rep hiring chain:

- The world's best sales rep recruitment method, the Virtual Bench;

- The world's most efficient tool to cut down the stack of resumes to just the ones you want to screen on the phone, the Topgrading Career History Form; and

- The best way to narrow the candidates on the phone, the Sales Representative Telephone Screen.

The Topgrading approach will save you a lot of time. We'll give you all the details, but most sales managers find that their time filling a job can be cut in half, saving about 10 hours.

Oh, and by the way, the Topgrading approach will fill those sales rep jobs with 80–90 percent high performers. It's faster and better.

Develop Your Virtual Bench

Running ads and paying recruiters are common recruiting methods, but the Virtual Bench technique is quicker because people are already prescreened, better because they are prescreened to be A players, and cheaper because there is no recruiter fee.

What's a Virtual Bench? When an athlete is tired, the coach will not call out to the fans, "Anyone want to play center?" The coach goes to the bench to put someone in who is a proven player. Your talent prospect list is your Virtual Bench—virtual because you haven't hired anyone on the list. You will need a constant flow of talented sales people coming your way, since there will always be turnover, most of which is due to poor sales performance.

Your Virtual Bench will consist of:

1. Ten actual sales rep prospects, and
2. Ten "connectors," sharp sales reps, managers, or others who would probably not join your team but who can recommend good sales people for you to recruit.

We know A player sales managers who devote about six hours every week to nurturing their Virtual Bench—e-mailing and calling people, having meals together, sending articles about some new sales idea—whatever it takes to keep sharp people interested.

At a conference, we observed one of the best practitioners of the Virtual Bench accept calls from his contacts during meals. He had to hire A players fast, and he said, "Telephone tag is a pain in the butt, and if people in my Virtual Bench struggle to stay in touch, they just won't do it." Being on call to your Virtual Bench at meals is a bit extreme, but you get the point.

Enlist all the A players in your company to create Virtual Benches. Also, as soon as you hire A players, ask them to give you the profiles of every A player they know. Keep a separate Rolodex for your

Virtual Bench, or use your PDA or address book with a special category for it.

Ann Drake, CEO of DSC Logistics, said, "We recruit all day, every day, with everyone we meet."

> *"We recruit all day, every day, with everyone we meet."*

Consider offering a bounty to anyone who can refer A player candidates. In one company, A players did not spend time producing candidates *until* they were offered the bounty. The average sales rep there earns $500,000; the sales manager now pays a $25,000 bounty—$5,000 when the rep is hired and $5,000 annually for four years. It works!

If you work in a big company, a terrific source is to ask customers who are the best sales people selling to them.

If yours is a midsize firm, hire from big companies: Target sales people who get great results but hate the bureaucracy, politics, and endless meetings. Stay in touch, and you'll hear when they've had it with their boss or some stupid policy. Then pounce!

If your company is small, you are short on resources, so your best source is apt to be your A players. Also, build your list of connectors by asking customers who the great sales people are, the reps who earn too much to join you but who may know less experienced people who *would* join you.

It has probably occurred to you that recruiting is a nonstop sales job in which you develop a fully functional Virtual Bench by doing what Ann Drake's team does: recruiting all day, every day, with everyone you meet.

Topgrading Career History Form

If you don't have a fully developed Virtual Bench, you'll be reviewing countless resumes—from ads, recruiters, and your Web site. It's hard cutting the stack of resumes from 150 to 30 because resumes are so deceptive. But you do it—Sunday afternoon, while trying to watch a sporting event on TV. Fun, huh?

Now you have a huge task—to call those 30 people and do a telephone screen. That could take weeks of telephone tag and consume 15–30 hours. The Topgrading Career History Form solves the problem. It's Appendix B, but here's what the first page looks like:

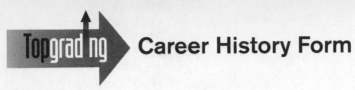 # Career History Form

This information will not be the only basis for hiring decisions. You are not required to furnish any information that is prohibited by federal, state, or local law.

Last name	First	Middle		
Home address	City	State	Zip code	Area code + telephone no. ( )
Business address	City	State	Zip code	Area code + telephone no. ( )
E-mail address	Mobile #		Date	

Position applied for _____ Earnings expected $ _____

I. Business Experience: *(Please start with your present or most recent position)*

A. Firm _____ Address _____
City _____ State _____ Zip_____ Phone _____
Kind of business_____ Starting date (mo/yr) _____ Final (mo/yr) _____
Title_____ Staff: Number of direct reports _____ Total Staff _____

Salary (Starting) [Base $ _____ Bonus $ _____ Other $ _____]
$ _____

Salary (Final) [Base $ _____ Bonus $ _____ Other $ _____]
$ _____

Name of immediate supervisor_____ Title _____
What do (did) you like most about your job? _____
What do (did) you least enjoy? _____
Reasons for leaving or desiring to change _____

B. Firm _____ Address _____
City _____ State _____ Zip_____ Phone _____
Kind of business_____ Starting date (mo/yr) _____ Final (mo/yr) _____
Title_____ Staff: Number of direct reports _____ Total Staff _____

The Topgrading Career History Form requires candidates to supply full compensation history (no resume contains that crucial information), months and years for every job (so a three-month job can't be excluded), and names of bosses (suggesting that you might contact those bosses). It provides 25 inches of space for a self-appraisal, asks what was liked and disliked about jobs, and includes a legal statement candidates must sign saying that if they lie, they can be fired (this inspires a higher level of honesty).

Just hand the 30 resumes to an assistant, who will e-mail the Topgrading Career History Form to all 30 with the following cover note:

Thank you for responding to our ad for Sales Representative. In order to continue the selection process, complete the enclosed form (all compensation information, please!) and e-mail it back.

A few days later, you'll have completed career history forms, and in one hour you'll sort through them and see maybe eight people you want to call. That one hour saved you at least 14 hours that it would have taken to call 30 people!

You can devise your own career history form or check out Topgrading resources in Chapter 6. The licensed version of the Topgrading Career History Form is most convenient because it can be e-mailed to candidates. You generally want to hire sales reps whose:

- Comp is increasing,

- Sales are of products or services similar to yours, and

- Tenure shows job stability.

From the information on the Topgrading Career History Form it's possible to summarize a person's career visually—a "snapshot."

Here is a Topgrading Snapshot of a sales rep whose pay declined during the 2000–2002 recession (OK, recessions happen) and who has hopped around from job to job since 2002, with declining pay. This is not the pattern of a winner!

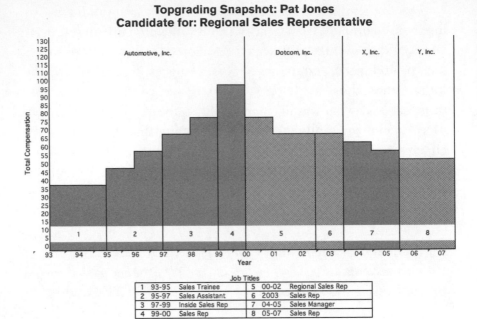

Topgrading Snapshot: Pat Jones
Candidate for: Regional Sales Representative

Job Titles

1	93-95	Sales Trainee	5	00-02	Regional Sales Rep
2	95-97	Sales Assistant	6	2003	Sales Rep
3	97-99	Inside Sales Rep	7	04-05	Sales Manager
4	99-00	Sales Rep	8	05-07	Sales Rep

Sales Representative Telephone Screen

Now you're ready to call the eight or so people whose resumes have been screened using the Topgrading Career History Form. Read the resume and Topgrading Career History Form, and then go through the telephone screen, cutting the interview short as soon as you determine you won't hire the person. But be nice, since sharp prospects can become part of your Virtual Bench.

The questions in the telephone screen zero in on what separates the best sales reps from the pack, so it's a productive use of time. The fifth variable in the SBI Formula for Sales Success is time, and time is fixed at 240 selling days per year. Using these precious days on the most revenue-producing activities is crucial. There are two kinds of selling activities: those that make money and those that don't make money directly but, if not done, can hurt sales. You want sales reps who are out with prospects and customers, making money, and doing their administrative chores after hours and on weekends.

The Sales Representative Telephone Screen elicits crucial information and eliminates poor candidates quickly. Sales Benchmark Index research indicates that a sales manager will conduct face-to-face interviews with 15 candidates for each rep hired using traditional hiring methods. The Topgrading Career History Form cuts a pack of 30 down to an average of eight people to talk with, and the telephone screen cuts the eight down to four face-to-face interviews.

Here are the Sales Representative Telephone Screen questions. After introducing yourself and explaining the job, ask about the present or most recent job:

1. **Please describe your territory.** Is the sales rep selling based on geography, product line, or names of accounts? Is he or she really on top of the territory?
2. **Please describe the quota system.** Is the candidate measured on revenue, gross profit, unit sales, new accounts, etc.? How well does the candidate explain the keys to success?
3. **Please describe your production.** Nail down performance vs. targets. How engaged is the person? Does he or she make excuses? Get answers to numbers 1–3 for more than the present job, perhaps the last three jobs, to perform a more thorough screen.
4. **Please describe your compensation plan.** Is there an understanding of how sales rep success drives company success? Is the person motivated?
5. **Please describe your company's value proposition.** This should be an "elevator pitch"—30 seconds.
6. **Please describe your major competitor's value proposition.** The differences between number 5 and number 6 should be very clear.
7. **Please explain the top three objections you must overcome to close sales . . . and how you overcome them.** Does the candidate beat the competition?

8. **Please describe your typical day and week.** Does the person work hard and work smart, doing administrative work after hours?

9. **What do you like most and least about your job?** Is the person a complainer? Would things be different in your company?

10. **Please describe what you like and dislike about your boss, and give your best guess as to what your boss would candidly tell me are your strengths, weaker points, and overall performance.** Do you fit the profile of what the candidate likes in a boss? Does he or she come from a competitive culture? Is the person honest or doing a whitewash?

Think of the sales rep hiring process as an inverted pyramid.

Sales Representative Hiring Pyramid

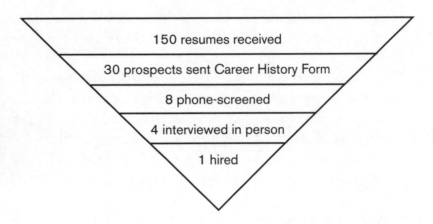

150 resumes received

30 prospects sent Career History Form

8 phone-screened

4 interviewed in person

1 hired

Now let's revisit the amount of time you can realistically save while hiring much better sales reps.

	Not Using Topgrading Career History Form	Using Career History Form
Number of Hours Phone-Screening Candidates	15	5

That's right, resumes are so incomplete and so often deceptive that it can take 15 hours on the phone to cut a stack of 30 resumes down to a few candidates to interview in person. But sales managers with completed Topgrading Career History Forms (and resumes) sort the wheat from the chaff, phone-screen only the few best candidates, and then meet the best of the best.

Although the Topgrading Career History Form is a huge time saver, it's not as good as recruiting from your Virtual Bench. Nothing beats hiring A players you know to be A players!

We hope you are getting the impression that in improving on all the links in the sales rep hiring chain, we are absolutely opposed to any bureaucratic, administrative, time-wasting bunk. Every link has been developed to save you time and save you the enormous costs of mis-hires, while helping you pack your sales force with better producers, who will guarantee that you will make your numbers.

CHAPTER 4

The Best Sales Rep Hiring Methods

This is the chapter with the silver bullet, the holy grail of hiring—the Topgrading Interview. First we'll outline the best hiring sequence, then share the essence of the Topgrading Interview, explain how to do reference checks that are actually useful, and finish with the Hiring Checklist, a handy reminder of all the steps taken by managers achieving 90 percent high performers hired.

To review, you have:

- Built the Sales Representative Scorecard;

- Performed the Sales Representative Talent Review;

- Analyzed the costs of mis-hires and potential shareholder benefits of Topgrading;

- Committed yourself to building a Virtual Bench to provide a steady stream of prescreened, likely A player prospects;

- Learned how use of the Topgrading Career History Form can save you a lot of time by cutting a stack of resumes down to just a few people to call; and

- Learned the ten questions to ask in a screening call that will sort the wheat from the chaff.

Now it's time to interview the three or four finalist candidates face-to-face.

The usual methods of interviewing candidates have been well researched, and the results are pathetic. "Tell me about yourself" interviews were replaced about 30 years ago with round-robin, 50-minute, competency (behavioral) interviews, which even C player sales candidates can easily fake.

Traditionally, HR and the hiring manager start by analyzing the job and writing a job scorecard, including about five competencies. The five competencies are to be scrutinized, one competency by each interviewer, and for a sales job they are obvious—selling skills, motivation, good work habits, etc. The typical questions are, "What example can you give me to show good work habits?" followed by, "What example can you give me of a time you could have demonstrated better work habits?" Duh! Candidates hype the positives and conceal the real negatives, confident that the only reference checking will be with the people they chose—neighbors, friends, priests, and their insurance sales rep. A survey of the number-one human resource executives from Global 100 companies, the largest in the world, showed that *most* used this hiring method, and they said the results are 80 percent mis-hires. Topgraders brag about only 10–20 percent mis-hires.

Lincoln Financial Group is a great Topgrading success story, with improved talent clearly helping to improve sales in its wholesale distribution group. Lincoln is the largest seller of life insurance and one of the largest sellers of annuities, in the United States. The sales force consists of wholesalers who sell to Merrill Lynch, UBS, Edward Jones, and similar companies. Terry Mullen took over a major sales channel when it was moved into the wholesaling business. He found that there were no quotas, and the hiring methods were quite shallow. What a great opportunity to Topgrade!

Terry introduced sales quotas, coached all the sales reps and held them accountable, and replaced about half of the team. Managers were replaced too. Topgrading methods were introduced. The Topgrading Career History Form was used to cut through piles of resumes, Virtual Benches were built up as A players came on board, and Topgrading Interviews were conducted with all finalists.

Topgrading is working! Two managers have been particularly effective Topgraders, with 89 percent of their combined 68 sales reps achieving goals in certain products. One manager has 100 percent of his 17 sales reps exceeding goals. Lincoln's Topgrading efforts in Sales is a "work in progress," and Terry is confident that 90 percent of the entire sales team will achieve the goals set for them.

Arrange Round-Robin Interviews

And now we'll surprise you. We encourage you to do round-robin competency interviews, although they achieve only about 25-percent hiring success. But you must add the Topgrading Interview and reference checks the way we recommend in order to double or triple your hiring success. Why do the round-robins? Sales reps, at least the A players, demand to interview with others on your team, and you want opinions from other interviewers. Fifty-minute interviews are not sufficient to hire well, but sales managers and sales candidates want multiple interviews, and the round-robin competency interviews are better than nothing.

We recommend four round-robin interviews, each focusing on one competency. You can generate your own questions, or you can take them from the back half of the Topgrading Interview Guide for Sales Representatives. It's a grocery list of competency ("behavioral") questions, so you can make up your own interview guide in minutes.

During the round-robin interviews, allow 15 minutes in which the *candidate* gets to ask the questions. Due diligence is a two-way street!

At the end of the day, convene a meeting of the four interviewers to get their opinions. If it's "thumbs up," arrange for a second visit for the Topgrading Interview.

Conduct the Topgrading Interview

Topgrading methods are all common sense—10 links in the hiring chain. If you skip even one, the cost will be your time and more mishires. You *must* conduct the Topgrading Interview, or the whole chain breaks. Sales managers can diligently apply all 10 methods and achieve 85-percent hiring success, but if they eliminate the Topgrading Interview, their success rate will drop precipitously.

Please read Appendix C, the Topgrading Interview Guide for Sales Representatives. You'll notice that it starts with Education and then moves to Work History, with the same 14 questions asked for every full-time job. Here is a simple, abbreviated version of the Topgrading Interview—"training wheels" for Topgrading. For every full-time job ask:

1. What were all of your accountabilities? (Quotas, etc.)
2. What were your successes and accomplishments? What are you proudest of? (Probe for *how* the successes were achieved.)
3. What were your failures and mistakes? Lessons learned? Excuses made? (Be sure answers to numbers 2 and 3 describe full performance against *all* accountabilities.)
4. Why did you leave?
5. Who was your boss, and where is that person now? What were his or her strengths and weaker points from your point of view? (Assess how well you, the interviewer, fit the profile the candidate likes.)
6. What's your best guess as to what your boss would tell me, in a personal reference interview arranged by you, were your strengths, weaker points, and overall performance?

> *Ask those six questions for every full-time job, and you will hire better.*

If you learn only one simple technique from this book, make it this one: Ask those six questions for every full-time job, and you will hire better.

How can we be so sure this interview method is valuable? Hundreds of people have asked for the "secret"—people sitting next to us on planes, golfing partners, and people we meet at parties. We both have scribbled these questions and said to ask candidates those questions for every full-time job. In return, we've asked that people e-mail us the results. In a few weeks, we get the e-mails or phone calls, and the message is always, "Wow! That was *by far* the best, most revealing, most worthwhile interview I've ever conducted!"

This might be the equivalent of saying to someone learning surgery, "Don't forget to slosh on the antiseptic." If the surgeon is merely doing two stitches but forgets the antiseptic, the patient could become infected, and the patient could die. Ditto for those six questions: Ask them and you'll hire better; if you don't ask them, you'll likely have a mis-hire.

Considering this Topgrading story:

Brad,

I stumbled on Topgrading near the end of 3.5 yrs as a sales manager. I had been gradually refining my own interview guide but was still getting too many false positives. Upon incorporating Topgrading, I avoided a number of costly mistakes and my last hiring decisions were much better than my prior decisions. Shortly after, I accepted an exciting opportunity that took me out of sales for over a year. However, my sales team continued to outperform the other sales teams and, even a full year after I had left sales, my people (distributed among the remaining teams) were collectively selling more than the salespeople hired by any of the remaining sales managers. Our Company has 30% annual turnover in Sales. So for every single person on my team to still be with the Company and performing well after a whole year suggests that I was doing something right in my hiring. Effective last week, I now have responsibility for all of Sales (2 sales managers and 20 salespeople). One of my first initiatives is to install Topgrading in our sales organization. My sales managers and I are excited by the results we expect.

Best,

Marcus E. Goormastic

This is all good news for you, the sales manager, for it will assure better hiring. But realistically, Topgrading is more than asking just these six questions for every job. To achieve 90-percent hiring success, you'll need to ask more than just those repeat six questions.

The first breakthrough in helping managers like you interview well was the invention of the Topgrading Interview Guide. It's a convenient "road map"—just ask the question, take notes, go on to the next question, take notes, and when all the questions on a page are asked and notes show the responses, turn the page. Easy!

We've designed the Topgrading Interview Guide for Sales Representatives so that every question is just the right question. The guide is very thorough and complete. It includes the competency questions (mostly to be used by round-robin interviewers) and a form at the back for rating competencies, organizing your conclusions, and deciding if this is an A player candidate. You can memorize the guide or purchase hard-copy or license online versions (see Chapter 6 for Topgrading resources).

We've referred to the first breakthrough (the Interview Guide), but what was the second? It's the use of *two* interviewers, the tandem Topgrading Interview. In the 1980s, Brad began consulting with General Electric, and CEO Jack Welch said, "Brad, the interview guide has definitely improved our batting average, but our managers don't get nearly the success we need. How can they do better?" Brad suggested the tandem approach, and Jack instantly agreed. A lot of companies copied GE's best practices, and today thousands of managers improve their hiring success by using an interview partner. All managers we know of who achieve 90 percent high performers hired used the tandem approach and the Topgrading Interview Guide.

How does a tandem interview work? Pick an A player and agree

> *All managers we know of who achieve 90 percent high performers hired used the tandem approach and the Topgrading Interview Guide.*

beforehand that one of you will be the primary interviewer, who asks most of the questions, keeps eye contact, and takes few notes, while the other will be the secondary interviewer, who takes a lot of notes and occasionally asks a question. Change the roles with each full-time job being discussed. Try the tandem approach, with both of you using the Topgrading Interview Guide, and you'll love it; it makes a very complex process so easy that truly 90 percent high performers can be hired.

How to Stay Out of a Minimum Security Prison

Fortunately, the Topgrading Interview Guide for Sales Representatives has been designed to minimize your risk of legal problems. Indeed, the largest employment law firm in the United States, Seyfarth Shaw, vetted all the components of Topgrading.* So stick to the interview guide, and you will be safe.

Unfortunately, you *can't* stick to the interview guide at all times. An interview is a dialogue, and you create a lot of follow-up questions to probe for specifics, clarify, and build rapport.†

If you ask questions that violate local, state, or federal laws, you might be charged with discriminatory practices. OK, you won't be visiting a minimum security prison, but we're sure you know of massive class-action financial penalties and court actions that require changes

---

* Seyfarth Shaw lawyers wrote Chapter 12, "Avoiding Legal Problems: A 'Bulletproof' Approach to Safe Hiring, Managing, and Firing Practices" in *Topgrading: How Leading Companies Win by Hiring, Coaching, and Keeping the Best People* (Portfolio, New York, 2005).

† To learn the best interviewing skills—how to create questions, build rapport, read body language—see the *Smart Interviewer: Tools and Techniques for Hiring the Best!* (Wiley, 1989).

in selection practices. Any sales manager charged with discriminatory practices faces a nightmare at best, including termination.

Our advice to you is to make a point of learning exactly what you can and cannot ask in interviews. Here's a primer. **Do *not* ask about:**

- Race

- Religion

- Age

- National origin

- Marital status

- Care for kids

- Pregnancy

- Arrest record

The spirit of the law is to make hiring fair, and the Equal Employment Opportunity Commission (EEOC) strongly encourages the methods Topgrading has had in place even prior to the creation of EEOC—job analysis, focus on measurable results, questions related to competencies, use of interview guides, note taking, etc. You are generally on safe ground if you think, *If it isn't job related, don't ask it!* And of course, if you aren't sure about what to do or what to ask in interviews, read up on the topic and check with HR or legal counsel.

> *If it isn't job related, don't ask it!*

Ask Candidates to Arrange Personal Reference Calls

This is an easy Topgrading innovation, and we've already mentioned it. In the 1980s, Brad was interviewing a candidate for VP Sales who said he talked with candidates' bosses. Asked how he was able to do it, he said, "I ask *candidates* to arrange reference calls." Bingo!

Today hundreds of companies use this technique, and over 90 percent of former bosses of A players take the reference call.

> Over 90 percent of former bosses of A players take the reference call.

Although companies tell managers *not* to take reference calls for fear that a negative reference might trigger a lawsuit, A players get their former bosses to talk. Those bosses aren't worried about a lawsuit, because they will say nice things about their former A players. C players can't get former bosses to talk—gee, we wonder why. A players are delighted to arrange for you to talk with bosses, because they figure you'll be impressed and maybe even offer a more attractive pay package.

Here's how to do it:

1. After the tandem Topgrading Interview, you and your partner decide whether you want to proceed or eliminate the candidate.
2. If you decide to conduct reference calls, the two of you look over your notes and decide which of the bosses, peers, or customers discussed are the ones you'd like to talk with. Most Topgraders want to talk with *all* bosses in the past decade.
3. Ask the candidate to call the people you've chosen, asking them to take a personal reference call, and then to report back to you the phone numbers and availability of the references.
4. Use the Topgrading Reference Check Guide for Sales Representatives (Appendix D). As with other forms and guides, memorize it if you do not have the budget to buy it. If you have more than 10 sales reps, consider purchasing all the guides in a package or licensing them (see Chapter 6, "Topgrading Resources").

You're done! Follow all of these steps, and with just a little practice, you'll develop confidence that you can be among the elite sales managers who hire not just 60 percent sales reps who make their numbers but 90 percent who exceed their quota and are truly A players. To be sure all of the important steps are taken, use the Hiring Checklist.

Hiring Checklist
for Sales Representatives

Date	
Candidate Name	
Job Title	
Hiring Manager	

☐ **Topgrading Sales Representative Scorecard Completed**
    ☐ Job-Specific Competencies
    ☐ Measurable Accountabilities

☐ **Topgrading Career History Form Completed**

☐ **Topgrading Interview Guide Completed**

Interviewer's Name _____ Date_____ Length_____
Interviewer's Name _____ Date_____ Length_____

☐ **Round-Robin Competency (Behavioral) Interviews**

    Interviewer's Name _____ Competency Examined _____
    Interviewer's Name _____ Competency Examined _____
    Interviewer's Name _____ Competency Examined _____
    Interviewer's Name _____ Competency Examined _____
    Interviewer's Name _____ Competency Examined _____

☐ **Reference Checks by Interviewer(s) (minimum: all bosses in past 10 years)**

    Interviewer's Name _____ Reference's Name/Title _____
    Interviewer's Name _____ Reference's Name/Title _____
    Interviewer's Name _____ Reference's Name/Title _____
    Interviewer's Name _____ Reference's Name/Title _____
    Interviewer's Name _____ Reference's Name/Title _____

☐ **Candidate Report**

    Executive Summary, Job-Specific Competencies Rated, Lists of Strengths, Weaker
    Points, and Developmental Suggestions

☐ **Job Offer Letter**

    Approval by _____ Date_____

CHAPTER 5

The Best Sales Rep
Coaching Methods

When you hire 90 percent A players, you certainly want to hang on to them! It's easier than you might think. Following all of the steps in Chapters 3 and 4, you'll have so much information regarding what will retain your A players that it will be hard for you *not* to keep them.

Onboarding is a fancy term for laying the groundwork in the first weeks so that your sales reps meet the right people inside the company and exposure to customers is planned and organized.

Since you have learned what transitioning to new jobs was like for every full-time job in the new hire's career, and since you scrutinized all aspects of every job, you'll know your new A player's strengths, weak points, industry knowledge, work habits . . . everything you need in order to plan the first few weeks.

Part of onboarding is continuing to recruit your new hire. Why? Many sales managers report that occasionally a new hire will continue interviewing for a better job. It's a huge embarrassment when a new hire keeps talking to other job prospects, bolts after a week or so, says adios, and takes a different job. Customers tend to wonder what your new superstar learned in the first couple of weeks that was so bad that it led to a hasty departure.

One of the biggest challenges in completing the onboarding process is coaching your sales people.

Coach Your Team of A Players

Hmm, you're thinking, *Maybe I'm not the world's best coach.* We have some good news, bad news, and then more good news for you.

First, the first good news: If you're not a super coach, you're in good company. We've surveyed over 1 million employees, and only 25 percent of managers, including sales managers, are rated Very Good or Excellent. Seventy-five percent are rated Very Poor, Poor, Only Fair, or Good. "Good" is lukewarm positive.

Why don't employees rate their managers better as coaches? Now the bad news: Employees say their managers are impatient, excessively demanding, hypercritical, too busy, stingy with positive feedback, and just not caring. Is that you?

The second good news here is the Topgrading bonus.

> *Hire A players and you automatically are a very good or excellent coach.*

Think for a minute. You're a much more positive, caring, patient coach to your A players, right? They smash their numbers, win customers over, and make you look good—and they are receptive to your suggestions. And of course they make *you* money. It's the C players who drag down your sales results, and sure enough, you are more negative with the sales reps who constantly let you down. They make excuses and are defensive when criticized. The main reason you're so demanding is because their results are so lousy!

The solution is to hire only A players. We've seen it in survey after survey—sales managers, *after* Topgrading a couple of years, show up as great coaches. They didn't attend any coaching workshops or have personality transplants. They just love having so many A players, and they *like* coaching them.

Coaching Guide

Here are our tips:

1. **Coach regularly.** Don't wait until a setback or an annual perform-ance appraisal. A players are eager for feedback and coaching, anything to help them succeed.
2. **Start coaching two weeks after your new A player comes on board.** The first page of the Topgrading Interview Guide for Sales Representatives promises feedback and coaching, and A players are not shy. "Hey, boss, you have a ton of information on me from my Career History Form, the round-robin interviews, the tandem Topgrading Interview, and all the reference check interviews I arranged, so coach me! Give me feedback and advice so I can be hugely successful."
3. **Create an Individual Development Plan.** Give your initial feed-back and advice to your newly hired A players, and ask *them* to write their IDP, saying what they intend to do, why, when, and how the results will be measured.
4. **Coach daily as needed, but formally on a quarterly basis.** Ask your A players to take the lead—to summarize their results and what they are doing to achieve them, what they are failing at and why (and how they'll fix it), how they are progressing on their IDP (and how they'd like to modify it), and finally, what they would like from you.

    A players are resourceful. They'll take the lead in their coach-ing sessions, and that's great! This approach is much healthier than the usual critical parent role taken by managers, in which they say a few positives and then nail their subordinate.
5. **Introduce your A players to the Sales Benchmark Index model.** Challenge them to be best in class on each variable and metric. (See Chapter 6 for information.)
6. **Allocate your time to coach your A players and those with A potential, with minimal coaching for your B and C players,**

those you are sure will *never* be high performers. Together we have assessed and coached more than 500 sales managers, and the best are Darwinian: They know that coaching can enable high performers to achieve even better results but that coaching chronic C players is useful mostly to give them a fair chance to succeed—but a lot of coaching can be a waste of time.

Nudge Out Your Low Performers

The 40-percent turnover in the sales ranks parallels the fact that 40 percent miss their sales targets annually. If you set the bar higher and expect far better results than industry standard, maybe 50–75 percent of your sales reps will fail. Coach and train all your hires, but when some

> *When some prove they are incapable of performing to your high expectations, let them fire themselves.*

prove they are incapable of performing to your high expectations, let them fire themselves. Occasionally there is another job in a large company where someone can leave a key account job and handle inside sales. Sales reps know the targets, and if they are falling short, you should have meetings to offer coaching, but when the coaching is clearly futile, nudge the person out.

Terminations usually involve a severance, and being terminated looks bad on someone's record. Low performers should not stick around until they are fired, because it's a lot easier to get a job when you have one. Chronic low performers lack resourcefulness in everything they do, including getting another job, so sometimes termination is necessary.

One of our favorite case studies is of Bob Dineen, who took over a low performing region for Merrill Lynch. (Bob is now an executive with Lincoln Financial.) He had 29 brokers, all low performing. These low performers were prominent in the community, so wholesale terminations would have made Merrill Lynch an outcast employer. Bob immediately began building his Virtual Bench, literally trying to have breakfasts and lunches with every high producing broker within 300 miles. He hired A players who blew away their peers, and he nudged out 27 of 29.

How did he do it? Creatively! He fired no one. His nudging was this: "Come to me monthly and rate yourself on a 10-point scale on effort and on attitude, and if either falls below 7, please leave. If I consider you below a 7 and you rate yourself above 7, your rating counts, and mine doesn't." It worked, and the office took off. The 27 departed brokers got other jobs, and Merrill Lynch enjoyed a great reputation in the community.

We're not recommending Bob's approach for you; after all, it gives too much power to underperformers. But Bob couldn't nudge faster without destroying Merrill Lynch's reputation. In most situations, it's better to have not just annual but quarterly goals. Failure to achieve those goals two quarters in a row might be enough to convince people that they won't achieve their annual goal, so leaving is best. It's generally best to cut your losses, to remove the hapless underperformers fast.

Enough negative talk! Hey, when you have 90 percent A players, the chronic Cs will bail out on their own, quickly, because they just won't fit in the positive, energized, resourceful culture of your A team.

Microsoft Case Study

Chris Jones is a relatively new general manager at Microsoft, with sales and marketing responsibility for a $500M business. He earned that level of responsibility in large part because of his success with his previous employer. In that job, he Topgraded his team, hiring 13 sales reps, and 85 percent have beaten stretch quotas for the past five years. As Chris notes, quotas in any given year might be too high or too low because of factors the rep can't control, but it becomes clear who the A players are when they beat quota year after year.

How exactly did Chris learn and apply Topgrading? He participated in a one-day Topgrading workshop, read the big *Topgrading* book, and began practicing all the Topgrading methods. He developed a Sales Rep Scorecard, improved his Virtual Bench, sent out the Topgrading Career History Form to cut the stack of resumes, used the Sales Representative Telephone Screen to decide whom to meet, used the Topgrading Interview Guide to assess finalists, and required candidates to arrange reference calls with various sales managers they had worked for. Round-robin competency interviews were conducted, each zeroing in on one particular sales competency. But as Chris put it,

> *Traditional competency interviews are of some value, but the interviewers can't completely connect the dots to arrive at really valid, accurate insights into the candidate. The Topgrading Interview and TORC Technique enabled me to double my hiring success.*

The TORC Technique? What's that? TORC stands for Threat of Reference Check, a very powerful incentive for interviewees to be totally honest and forthcoming in interviews and not try to hide information or "spin" failures. Here's how it works: just inform candidates that in order to get a job *they* will, at a late stage in the hiring process, contact bosses they've had in the past decade and arrange for them to speak to the hiring manager or a tandem interviewer. When candidates hear that, C players are scared off and A players are attracted.

During the Tandem Topgrading Interview a candidate is asked to appraise every boss and guess what bosses will say in reference interviews arranged by that candidate, how each boss will describe their strengths, weak points, and overall performance. Candidates know they had better tell the whole truth or else the reference calls they arrange will show they are fudging the truth, not in tune with bosses, or both. That genuine threat of reference checks (TORC Technique) is only a threat to C players; A players *want* prospective employers to talk to their bosses, to hear how terrific they are.

Chris didn't use the tandem Topgrading Interview approach, in part because that method was not strongly encouraged until the

2005 version of *Topgrading*. Perhaps his results would have been even better if he had teamed up with an interviewing partner. We have found that some sales managers become terrific Topgrading interviewers on their own and really don't need a partner. Those sales managers have conducted over 100 Topgrading Interviews, and when they conduct tandem interviews, it's mostly to help train their interviewing partner. Our recommendation to you is to start with the tandem approach, and if you get to be so good that your partners do not offer sufficient value to be included, and if 90 percent of your sales reps turn out to be A players, go solo.

CHAPTER 6

How to Get Started: Topgrading Resources

Use the methods and tools in Chapters 1–5, and you will *at least* double your hiring success. If 40 percent of your sales reps miss industry-average quota, the Topgrading methods already covered in this book should cut your failures in half, to 20 percent.

Here's a summary of steps you can take now to double your hiring success without using any additional Topgrading tools:

1. Construct a Topgrading Scorecard for Sales Representatives, so you know what job you are really hiring for (see page 55).
2. Analyze your team, using the Annual Talent Review Form, to nail down who are your keepers and who are not. Nudge out the nots (see page 14).
3. Analyze a few of your past and all future mis-hires, using the Sales Representative Cost of Mis-Hires Form, to fully understand how costly it is *not* to Topgrade (see page 16).
4. Develop your Virtual Bench, your list of prospects and connectors to call, so that you rarely have to resort to running ads or paying recruiters.
5. Use the Topgrading Career History Form and Sales Representative Telephone Screen questions to save about 10 hours each time you select a sales rep (see pages 58 and 31).
6. Use round-robin competency interviews to screen finalist candidates (see page 75).
7. Memorize the six most basic Topgrading Interview questions, and ask sales candidates those six questions for all full-time jobs,

in order to gain the deepest insights into your finalists, for *all* crucial competencies (see page 62).

8. Ask finalist candidates to arrange reference calls with bosses in the past decade, both to get reference opinions *and* to motivate candidates to be honest in interviews (see page 93).

9. Coach your sales reps regularly. Ask each to create an Individual Development Plan, and follow up on it quarterly to ensure that your reps will perform at their peak.

10. Subscribe to the free monthly Topgrading newsletter, *Topgrading Tips,* at www.SmartTopgrading.com, for regular tips on how to create a top sales team.

    While you are at this Web site, read the free Press and Articles sections for additional practical tips.

Topgrading Tips

Resources

New 1-Hour Video on Interviewing and Hiring

Topgrading Shop

Consulting Services

Workshops and Speeches

Topgrading Articles

Contact Us

For the latest Topgrading news, articles, tools, and services, click here or go to: www.SmartTopgrading.com

New Blog!

For frequent short commentary plus library of Topgrading Tips, click here or go to: Blog.SmartTopgrading.com

Most Personality Tests are Shams

We get lots of questions about testing, because clients would love to have some sort of inexpensive screening device that cuts the candidate pool down to just a few to call and then to interview. Unfortunately, the fact is that most personality tests are validated in a devious way that makes the tests look useful, when they are not. I'll explain why:

I have on my desk the validation manual for one of the many personality tests used to screen candidates for sales positions. It's a thick manual. When the test is "tested," it's administered to *present* employees, with the promise that their score will *not* be known to their employer. OK, so the current employees have no motivation to fake answers; they are honest, and so sales people might admit they are not highly motivated, that they call on present customers when they should call prospects, etc. Then the test purveyors match the results against performance and, VOILÁ, the people who sell the most are the ones with the highest test scores. The test appears valid! But it's *not.*

Subscribe to receive the free quarterly Sales Benchmark Index (SBI) World Class 100 Report at www.salesbenchmarkindex.com for insights into hiring trends being adopted by the world's top performing sales organizations.

Sales Benchmarking

Sales Management Tips   **February 2007**

In This Issue

Sales Benchmarking - Finding and Then Fixing What's Wrong in Your Sales Organization

The Largest Hidden Cost In Sales

Why You Should Introduce Science into Sales Management

Quick Links

Benchmarking Blog
Benchmarking Articles
How To Benchmark
Benchmarking Inventory
Register Now

Welcome to the Sales Benchmarking Newsletter where you will receive the latest sales management tips and updates from the Sales Benchmark Index.

Yours In Battle,

The Sales Benchmark Index Team
www.salesbenchmarkindex.com
gethelp@salesbenchmarkindex.com
888.556.7338

How to Improve from Hiring 50 Percent to Hiring 80 or 90 Percent A Player Sales Reps

Maybe you should hit a few singles and doubles first. Try the Topgrading methods, and enjoy success. Then learn how to hit the ball out of the park.

So far this book promises to enable you to achieve 80-percent successful hiring, when success is defined as meeting industry average quotas. But suppose your performance bar is higher. To become a full-blown, certifiable Topgrader, you must achieve 90-percent hiring success, with success defined as achieving stretch goals, quotas far above industry standard.

To achieve superior results, you will probably want to use the videos, guides, workshops, and other resources developed to help.

When you are ready, go to www.SmartTopgrading.com, and then click on the Topgrading Shop. There you'll see tools developed recently to help managers—videos, books, and both hard-copy and licensed e-versions of the forms and guides.

Ask us your questions. We'll always give you our best advice! Our contact information is:

Brad: Brad.Smart@Topgrading.com

Greg: Greg.Alexander@SalesBenchmarkIndex.com

Appendix A

 **Scorecard**
for Sales Representatives

Candidate Name	
Title	
Company Name	
Date	
Rating (A, B, C)	
Recommendation	

Situation Description
Mission of the Role

The core mission of the role of Sales Representative for ABC Company is to grow revenue from the assigned territory by 20 percent. The revenue production will come from the opening of new accounts through executing against the company's designed sales process. ABC Company uses Sales Benchmark Index's Formula for Sales Success. The role of a Sales Representative for ABC Company is to achieve best-in-class status for each variable of the sales formula.

SBI's Formula for Sales Success

Targeted Compensation Range (external candidates only):
- Base: $75,000
- Commission: $75,000
- OTE (On-Target Earnings): $150,000

Selling Points (external candidates only):
- Large territory
- Uncapped compensation plan
- Strong demand for new products
- Properly set quota
- Seasoned district sales manager as supervisor

Key Accountabilities

Accountabilities	Importance (H, M, L)	Rating and Comments
1. Revenue: Exceed annual revenue quota of $1.0M.	H	
2. Activities: Maintain an activity level of seven sales calls per week.	M	
3. Conversions: Build pipeline-to-quota ratio of 5:1.	M	
4. Transactions: Sell each deal with a selling price at or above company averages.	M	
5. Talent: Consistently rank in the top 20 percent of performers across company sales force.	M	
6. Time: Spend 240 selling days out of the fiscal year's 260 in the field with prospects.	M	

Competency Scorecard

Competency	Rating and Comments (6=Excellent, 1=Poor)
SELLING SKILLS	
1. Track record	
2. Phone selling skills	
3. E-mail prospecting	
4. Closing ability	
5. Objection handling, cost justification	
6. Negotiating	
7. Capitalizing on marketing programs	
8. Generating referrals	
9. Leveraging leads	
10. Time management—capitalizing on peak selling hours	
11. Managing sales-support resources	

Competency	Rating and Comments (6=Excellent, 1=Poor)
KNOWLEDGE	
12. Experience	
13. Territory knowledge	
14. Technology tools	
15. Pricing methods	
16. Margin analysis	
17. Learning new products	
18. Converting strategy to tactics	
19. Written communication, proposal quality	
PERSONAL ATTRIBUTES	
20. Integrity	
21. Self-awareness	
22. Winning personality	
23. Enthusiasm	
24. Hard work, motivation, energy	
25. Team player	
26. First impression	
27. Risk taking	
28. Judgment	
29. Resourcefulness	
ADDITIONAL COMPETENCIES	
30.	
31.	
32.	
33.	

Appendix B

 **Career History Form**

This information will not be the only basis for hiring decisions. You are not required to furnish any information that is prohibited by federal, state, or local law.

Last name	First	Middle			
Home address	City	State	Zip code	Area code + telephone no. ( )	
Business address	City	State	Zip code	Area code + telephone no. ( )	
E-mail address	Mobile #		Date		

Position applied for _____ Earnings expected $_____

I. Business Experience: *(Please start with your present or most recent position)*

A. Firm _____ Address _____
City _____ State _____ Zip_____ Phone _____
Kind of business_____ Starting date (mo/yr) _____ Final (mo/yr) _____
Title_____ Staff: Number of direct reports _____ Total Staff _____

Salary (Starting)
$ _____
⎡ Base $ _____
⎢ Bonus $ _____
⎣ Other $ _____ ⎤

Salary (Final)
$ _____
⎡ Base $ _____
⎢ Bonus $ _____
⎣ Other $ _____ ⎤

Name of immediate supervisor_____ Title _____
What do (did) you like most about your job? _____
What do (did) you least enjoy? _____
Reasons for leaving or desiring to change _____

B. Firm _____ Address _____
City _____ State _____ Zip_____ Phone _____
Kind of business_____ Starting date (mo/yr) _____ Final (mo/yr) _____
Title_____ Staff: Number of direct reports _____ Total Staff _____

Salary (Starting)
$ _____

[Base $ _____
Bonus $ _____
Other $ _____]

Salary (Final)
$ _____

[Base $ _____
Bonus $ _____
Other $ _____]

Name of immediate supervisor _____ Title _____

What do (did) you like most about your job? _____

What do (did) you least enjoy? _____

Reasons for leaving or desiring to change _____

C. Firm _____ Address _____

City _____ State _____ Zip _____ Phone _____

Kind of business _____ Starting date (mo/yr) _____ Final (mo/yr) _____

Title _____ Staff: Number of direct reports _____ Total Staff _____

Salary (Starting)
$ _____

[Base $ _____
Bonus $ _____
Other $ _____]

Salary (Final)
$ _____

[Base $ _____
Bonus $ _____
Other $ _____]

Name of immediate supervisor _____ Title _____

What do (did) you like most about your job? _____

What do (did) you least enjoy? _____

Reasons for leaving or desiring to change _____

Previous Positions Held

	a. Company b. City	a. Your title b. Name of supervisor	Date (mo/yr) a. Began b. Left	Compensation a. Initial b. Final	a. Type of work b. Reason for leaving
D. a.				$	
b.				$	
E. a.				$	
b.				$	
F a.				$	
b.				$	
G. a.				$	
b.				$	
H. a.				$	
b.				$	
I. a.				$	
b.				$	
J. a.				$	
b.				$	

Indicate by letter _____ *any of the above employers you do not wish contacted.*

II. Military Experience:

If in service, indicate branch _____

Date (mo/yr) entered _____ Date (mo/yr) discharged _____

Nature of duties _____

Highest rank or grade _____ Terminal rank or grade _____

III. Education:

High School 1 2 3 4   College/Graduate School 1 2 3 4 5 6 7 8   *(Circle highest grade completed)*

High School   Name of High School _____ Location _____

Approximate number in graduating class _____ Rank from the top _____

Final grade-point average _____ (A = ___)

Extracurricular activities _____

_____

Offices, honors, and awards _____

Part-time and summer work _____

COLLEGE/GRADUATE SCHOOL

Name and location	Dates From	To	Degree	Major	Grade-Point Average	Total Credit Hours	Extracurricular activities, honors, and awards
					(A = __)		
					(A = __)		
					(A = __)		

What undergraduate courses did you like most? Why?_____

What undergraduate courses did you like least? Why?_____

How was your education financed? _____

Part-time and summer work _____

Other courses, seminars, or studies _____

IV. Activities:

Membership in professional or job-relevant organizations (You may exclude groups that indicate race, color, religion, national origin, disability, or other protected status.)

_____

Publications, patents, inventions, professional licenses, or additional special honors or awards _____

What qualifications, abilities, and strong points will help you succeed in this job? _____

_____

What are your weak points and areas for improvement? _____

_____

V. Career Needs:

Willing to relocate? **Yes** _____ **No** _____ If no, explain _____

Amount of overnight travel acceptable ___ _____

What are your career objectives? _____

_____

VI. Other:

Do you have the legal right to work for any employer in the United States? **Yes** __ **No** __
Would you be willing to arrange reference calls with supervisors you've had in the past decade, as a last step before a final job offer? **Yes** _____ **No** _____

I certify that answers given in this Topgrading Career History Form are true, accurate and complete to the best of my knowledge. I authorize investigation into all statements I have made on this Form as may be necessary for reaching an employment decision. I understand that I may be asked to arrange reference calls with managers I've worked for.

In the event I am employed, I understand that any false or misleading information I knowingly provided in my Career History Form or interview(s) may result in discharge and/or legal action. I understand that if employed, I am required to abide by all rules and regulations of the employer and any special agreements reached between the employer and me. _____   _____

SIGNATURE   DATE

Please return this form to the company requesting its completion, *not* to Smart & Associates, Inc.

SMART & ASSOCIATES, INC.
37202 North Black Velvet Lane
Wadsworth, IL 60083
Phone: 847-244-5544 Fax: 847-263-1585
1998 © Smart & Associates, Inc., revised 2007
www.SmartTopgrading.com

Interview Guide
for Sales Representatives

Applicant	
Interviewer	
Date	

2007 © Smart & Associates, Inc.

"There is something that is much more scarce, something finer far, something rarer than ability.
It is the ability to recognize ability."
—Elbert Hubbard

This guide seeks to provide you with *the* most accurate, most valid insights when assessing internal talent and candidates to hire. Companies can achieve a record of 90 percent success hiring A players when a tandem Topgrading Interview (two interviewers) is conducted and the interviewers have been trained in the Topgrading Interview techniques.

Maximum benefits in using this Topgrading Interview Guide can be achieved through applying the principles stated in the book *Topgrading: How Leading Companies Win By Hiring, Coaching, and Keeping A Players,* by Bradford D. Smart Ph.D. (Portfolio, New York, 2005) and *Topgrading for Sales* by Bradford D. Smart, Ph.D., and Greg Alexander (Portfolio, New York, 2008).

This guide is intended to make the interviewer's job easier. It is a comprehensive, chronological guide, providing plenty of space to record responses. Experience has shown the following guidelines to be helpful when interviewing selection candidates:

1. Review the candidate's **Topgrading Career History Form** and **resume.**

2. Be sure that the **Job Scorecard, competencies, and first-year accountabilities** (quotas, etc.) are clear to you and the team the successful candidate will work with.

3. Review this guide prior to the interview, in order to:
   - **Refresh your memory** regarding the sequence and wording of questions, for a smoother interview.
   - **Add or delete questions** based upon what previous information (resume, Career History Form, preliminary interviews, reference checks) have disclosed about the individual.

4. Use a **tandem** (two-interviewer) approach.
A tandem interview is more valid than a solo interview, unless the Topgrading interviewer is highly experienced. Two heads are truly better than one when asking the Topgrading Interview questions, analyzing the interview responses, arriving at conclusions, and providing useful feedback and coaching.

5. After a couple of minutes building rapport, give the interviewee an idea of the expected time frame (three hours?) and then *sell* the person on being open and honest. For an external candidate for hire, you might state *purposes* such as to:
   - "Review your **background, interests, and goals** to see if there is a good match with the position and opportunities here."
   - "Determine some ways to assure **your smooth assimilation** into your new position, should you join us."
   - "Get some ideas regarding what you and we can do to maximize your **long-range fulfillment and contributions.**"
   - "Tell you more about the **career opportunities** we have to offer and answer any questions you have."
   - "**Understand your career history**, which will be thoroughly verified in **reference checks** we'll ask *you* to arrange with a minimum of all bosses you've had in the past ten years."

6. Following the Topgrading Interview:
   - **Review** the completed guide.
   - Conduct in-depth **reference checks** (arranged by the candidate), and accumulate opinions from coworkers who conducted interviews with the person.
   - **Write comments** about each competency on the last three pages of this guide.
   - **Make final ratings** of the competencies.

7. **Write a brief report**—an executive summary, followed by a list of strengths, weak points, and developmental recommendations.

College

So that I can get a good feel for your background, first your education and then work experience, let's *briefly* go back to your college days and come forward chronologically, up to the present. Then we'll talk about your plans and goals for the future.

Note to interviewers: Start with college or first full-time job, whichever came first.

1. I see from the Career History Form (or Self-Administered Topgrading Interview Guide) that you **attended** _____(college). Would you please expand on the information provided and give me a **brief rundown** on your college years, particularly events that might have affected later career decisions. We'd be interested in knowing about **work experiences**, what the school was like, what you were like back then, the curriculum, activities, how you did in school, high and low points, and so forth. (Ask the following questions to obtain complete information not included in responses to the general "smorgasbord" question.)

2. Give us a feel for **what kind of school** it was (if necessary, specify large/small, rural/urban, cliquish, etc.) and generally what your college years were like. _____
_____

3. What was your **major**? (Did you change majors?) _____
_____
_____

4. What school **activities** did you take part in? (Note activities listed on Career History Form, and get elaboration.) _____
_____

5. What sort of **grades** did you receive, what was your class standing, and what were your study habits like? (Confirm data on Career History Form.)
        GPA: _____/_____(scale)
        Study Habits _____

6. What **people or events** during college might have had an influence on your career?_____
_____
_____

7. Were there any class **offices, awards, honors,** or **special achievements** during your college years? (Note Topgrading Career History Form responses, and get elaboration.) _____

_____

_____

_____

8. What were **high points** during your college years? (Look for leadership, any sales successes, resourcefulness, and particularly what competencies the interviewee exhibits *now* while discussing those years.) _____

_____

_____

_____

9. What were **low points,** or **least enjoyable occurrences,** during your college years? (Again, what happened back then is only important in relation to what is revealed about the interviewee *now*.) _____

_____

_____

_____

10. Give us a feel for any **jobs** you held during college—the types of jobs, whether they were during the school year or summer, hours worked, and any high or low points associated with them. (Don't spend much time on these jobs, but look for indications of extraordinary resourcefulness, sales ability, motivation, etc.; if the person did not work during the summer, ask how the summer months were spent.)_____

_____

_____

_____

11. (Transition Question) What were your **career thoughts** toward the end of college?_____

_____

_____

_____

Work History

Ask all 14 questions about *every* full time job, starting with the very first one. Come forward chronologically and spend the most time on the most recent jobs. If the person recently worked for a single employer and had, say, three jobs of two years each with that employer, consider each one of those a *separate* position and complete a Work History Form on it.

1. What was the name of the **employer**, **location**, and **dates** of employment? (Get a feel for the organization by asking about revenues, products/services, number of employees, etc.)
2. What was your job **title**?
3. What were the starting and final levels of **compensation**? (base, bonus, other)
4. What were your **expectations** for the job?
5. What were your **responsibilities and accountabilities**? What were specific quotas or goals for revenue growth, margins, acquisition of new customers, etc.?
6. What did you **find** when you arrived? What shape was the job in—resources, problems? What major **challenges** did you face?
7. What results were achieved in terms of **successes and accomplishments**? How were they achieved? (As time permits, get specifics, such as individual vs. shared accomplishments, barriers overcome, bottom-line results, and impact on career—bonus, promotability, performance review.) Pin down performance in relation to quotas and other accountabilities (question number 5).
8. We all make **mistakes.** What would you say were mistakes or failures experienced in this job? If you could wind the clock back, what would you do differently?
9. All jobs seem to have their pluses and minuses; what were the **most enjoyable** or rewarding aspects of this job?
10. What were the **least enjoyable** aspects of the job?
11. What **circumstances** contributed to your **leaving**? (Always probe for initially unstated reasons.)
12. What was your **supervisor's name** and title? **Where** is that person now? Would you be willing to arrange for us to talk with him or her? (Say you will want to talk with all supervisors in the past ten years.)
13. What is/was it like working for him or her, and what were his or her **strengths** and **shortcomings** as a supervisor, from your point of view?
14. What is your **best guess** as to what (supervisor's name) honestly felt were/are your **strengths, weak points,** and **overall performance** (rated on a scale of excellent, good, fair, poor)?

Work History Form 1

1. _____

    Employer   Starting Date (mo./yr.)   Final (mo./yr.)

    _____

    Location   Type of Business

    _____

    Description of Company

2. Title _____

3.

Salary   ⎡ Base   \$ _____ ⎤   Salary   ⎡ Base   \$ _____ ⎤
(Starting) | Bonus   \$ _____ | (Final) | Bonus   \$ _____ |
\$ _____ ⎣ Other   \$ _____ ⎦   \$ _____ ⎣ Other   \$ _____ ⎦

4. Expectations _____

5. Responsibilities/Accountabilities _____
_____

6. "Found" (Major Challenges) _____

7. Successes/Accomplishments (How achieved?)_____

8. Failures/Mistakes (Why?) (Do differently?)_____
_____

9. Most enjoyable _____
10. Least enjoyable _____
11. Reasons for Leaving _____

Supervisor

12. _____

    Supervisor's Name   Title

    _____

    Where Now   Permission to contact?

13. Appraisal of Supervisor: His/Her Strengths_____
His/Her Shortcomings _____

14. Best guess as to what he/she really felt at that time were **your** strengths, weak points, and overall performance rating:

Strengths	Weak Points

    Overall Performance Rating _____

Work History Form 2

1. _____

    Employer   Starting Date (mo./yr.)   Final (mo./yr.)

    _____

    Location   Type of Business

    _____

    Description of Company

2. Title _____

3.

Salary   ⎡ Base $ _____ ⎤   Salary   ⎡ Base $ _____ ⎤
(Starting) | Bonus $ _____ | (Final) | Bonus $ _____ |
$ _____ ⎣ Other $ _____ ⎦ $ _____ ⎣ Other $ _____ ⎦

4. Expectations _____

5. Responsibilities/Accountabilities _____

6. "Found" (Major Challenges) _____

7. Successes/Accomplishments (How achieved?) ___

8. Failures/Mistakes (Why?) (Do differently?) ___

9. Most Enjoyable_____

10. Least Enjoyable _____

11. Reasons for Leaving _____

Supervisor

12. _____

    Supervisor's Name   Title

    _____

    Where Now   Permission to contact?

13. Appraisal of Supervisor: His/Her Strengths _____
       His/Her Shortcomings _____

14. Best guess as to what he/she really felt at that time were **your** strengths, weak points, and overall performance rating:

Strengths	**Weak Points**

    Overall Performance Rating _____

Work History Form 3

1. _____

   Employer   Starting Date (mo./yr.)   Final (mo./yr.)

   _____   _____

   Location   Type of Business

   _____

   Description of Company

2. Title _____

3.

Salary   ⎡Base $ _____⎤   Salary   ⎡Base $ _____⎤
(Starting)   ⎢Bonus $ _____⎢   (Final)   ⎢Bonus $ _____⎢
$ _____   ⎣Other $ _____⎦ $ _____ ⎣Other $ _____⎦

4. Expectations _____

5. Responsibilities/Accountabilities _____

6. "Found" (Major Challenges) _____

7. Successes/Accomplishments (How achieved?) _____

8. Failures/Mistakes (Why?) (Do differently?) _____

9. Most Enjoyable _____
10. Least Enjoyable _____
11. Reasons for Leaving _____

Supervisor

12. _____

   Supervisor's Name   Title

   _____

   Where Now   Permission to contact?

13. Appraisal of Supervisor: His/Her Strengths _____
      His/Her Shortcomings _____

14. Best guess as to what he/she really felt at that time were **your** strengths, weak points, and overall performance rating:

Strengths	Weak Points

Overall Performance Rating _____

Work History Form 4

1. _____

Employer   Starting Date (mo./yr.)   Final (mo./yr.)

_____

Location   Type of Business

_____

Description of Company

2. Title _____

3.

Salary (Starting)   [Base $ _____   Salary (Final)   [Base $ _____
               Bonus $ _____   Bonus $ _____
$ _____   Other $ _____] $ _____   Other $ _____]

4. Expectations _____

5. Responsibilities/Accountabilities _____

_____

6. "Found" (Major Challenges) _____

_____

7. Successes/Accomplishments (How achieved?) _____

_____

8. Failures/Mistakes (Why?) (Do differently?) _____

9. Most Enjoyable _____

10. Least Enjoyable _____

11. Reasons for Leaving _____

Supervisor

12. _____

Supervisor's Name   Title

_____

Where Now   Permission to contact?

13. Appraisal of Supervisor: His/Her Strengths _____
His/Her Shortcomings _____

14. Best guess as to what he/she really felt at that time were **your** strengths, weak points, and overall performance rating:

Strengths	Weak Points

Overall Performance Rating _____

Work History Form 5

1. _____

    Employer   Starting Date (mo./yr.)   Final (mo./yr.)

_____

    Location   Type of Business

_____

    Description of Company

2. Title _____

3.

Salary (Starting)   Base $ _____   Salary (Final)   Base $ _____

$ _____   Bonus $ _____ $ _____   Bonus $ _____

    Other $ _____   Other $ _____

4. Expectations _____

5. Responsibilities/Accountabilities _____

6. "Found" (Major Challenges) _____

7. Successes/Accomplishments (How achieved?) _____

8. Failures/Mistakes (Why?) (Do differently?) _____

9. Most Enjoyable _____
10. Least Enjoyable _____
11. Reasons for Leaving _____

Supervisor

12. _____

    Supervisor's Name   Title

_____

    Where Now   Permission to contact?

13. Appraisal of Supervisor: His/Her Strengths _____
His/Her Shortcomings _____

14. Best guess as to what he/she really felt at that time were **your** strengths, weak points, and overall performance rating:

Strengths	Weak Points

Overall Performance Rating _____

Work History Form 6

1. _____

    Employer   Starting Date (mo./yr.)   Final (mo./yr.)

 _____

    Location   Type of Business

 _____

    Description of Company

2. Title _____

3.

Salary (Starting)	Base	$ _____	Salary (Final)	Base	$ _____
	Bonus	$ _____		Bonus	$ _____
$ _____	Other	$ _____	$ _____	Other	$ _____

4. Expectations _____

5. Responsibilities/Accountabilities _____

_____

6. "Found" (Major Challenges) _____

7. Successes/Accomplishments (How achieved?) _____

_____

8. Failures/Mistakes (Why?) (Do differently?) _____

_____

9. Most Enjoyable _____

10. Least Enjoyable _____

11. Reasons for Leaving _____

Supervisor

12. _____

    Supervisor's Name   Title

 _____

    Where Now   Permission to contact?

13. Appraisal of Supervisor: His/Her Strengths _____

    His/Her Shortcomings _____

14. Best guess as to what he/she really felt at that time were **your** strengths, weak points, and overall performance rating:

Strengths	Weak Points

Overall Performance Rating _____

Plans and Goals for the Future

1. Let's discuss what you are looking for in your **next job**. (Note Career Needs section of Topgrading Career History Form.)

_____
_____
_____
_____

2. What are **other job possibilities**, and how do you feel about each one?

_____
_____
_____
_____

3. Describe your **ideal position** and what makes it ideal.

_____
_____
_____
_____

4. How does **this opportunity** square with your ideal position? What do you view as opportunities and advantages as well as risks and disadvantages in joining us?

Advantages _____
_____

Disadvantages _____
_____

Self-Appraisal

1. We would like you to give us a thorough **self-appraisal**, beginning with what you consider your **strengths, assets**, things you **like about yourself**, and things you **do well**.

2. OK, let's look at the other side of the ledger for a moment. What would you say are your **shortcomings, weak points,** or **areas for improvement?**

Self-Appraisal

Strengths	Weak Points

Specific Competencies for Sales Representatives

The following questions are optional in the Topgrading Interview. Those with an asterisk (*) are usually asked, unless they have been answered in the chronological portion of the Topgrading Interview. Get specific examples, not general responses.

These questions can also be used by interviewers performing one-hour competency-based interviews.

Selling Skills Competencies

1. Selling Skills

    a. Please describe your **sales approach** in detail_____

_____

_____

If candidate does not provide information about the following components of selling skills, ask for a description:

    b. Phone Selling Skills _____

_____

    c. Active Listening _____

_____

    d. E-mail Prospecting _____

_____

    e. Closing Ability _____

_____

    f. Objection Handling _____

_____

    g. Cost Justifying _____

_____

    h. Negotiating _____

_____

    i. Retaining Customers _____

_____

j. Capitalizing on Marketing Programs _____

_____

k. Generating Referrals _____

_____

l. Leveraging Leads _____

_____

m. Capitalizing on Peak Selling Hours _____

_____

n. Managing Sales Support Resources _____

_____

Sales Knowledge Competencies

2. Sales Knowledge

a. Please summarize the highlights and low lights of your sales **track record**—your successes and failures. _____

_____

If candidate does not provide sufficient information about the following knowledge categories, compose a question about:

b. Territory Knowledge _____

_____

c. Pricing Methods _____

_____

d. Margin Analysis _____

_____

e. Learning New Products _____

_____

f. Converting Strategy to Tactics _____

_____

g. Proposal Quality (ask for samples) _____

_____

Intellectual Competencies

3. Intelligence

a. Please describe your **learning ability.** _____

_____

b. Describe a **complex situation in** which you had to learn a lot, quickly. How did you go about learning, and how successful were the outcomes? _____

_____

4. Analysis Skills

a. Please describe your **problem analysis** skills. _____

_____

b. Do people generally regard you as one who diligently pursues every **detail,** or do you tend to be more **broad brush?** Why? _____

_____

c. What will references indicate are your style and overall effectiveness in **sorting** the wheat from the chaff? _____

_____

d. What **analytic approaches** and tools do you use? _____

_____

e. Please give me an example of **digging** more **deeply** for facts than was asked of you. _____

_____

5. Judgment/Decision Making

* **a.** Please describe how your **decision-making** approach, when you are faced with difficult situations, has changed in recent years. Are you more decisive and quick, but sometimes too quick, or are you more thorough but sometimes too slow? Are you more intuitive or less? Do you involve more or fewer people in decisions? _____

_____

b. What are a couple of the **most difficult** or **challenging** decisions you have made recently? _____

_____

c. What are a couple of the **best** and **worst** decisions you have made in the past year? _____

_____

d. What **maxims** do you live by? _____

_____

6. Conceptual Ability

Are you more comfortable dealing with concrete, tangible, short-term issues or more abstract, **conceptual** long-term issues? Please explain. _____

_____

_____

7. Creativity

* **a.** How **creative** are you? What are the best examples of your creativity in processes, systems, methods, products, structure, or services?

_____

_____

b. Do you consider yourself a better **visionary** or implementer, and why? _____

_____

_____

8. Strategic Skills

* **a.** In the past year, what specifically have you done in order to remain **knowledgeable** about the competitive environment, market and trade dynamics, products/services and technology trends, innovations, and patterns of consumer behavior? _____

_____

_____

b. Please describe your experience in **strategic planning**, including successful and unsuccessful approaches. (Determine the individual's contribution in team strategic efforts.) _____

_____

c. Where do you predict that your (**industry/competitors/function**) **will go** in the next three years? What is the **conventional wisdom**, and what are your own thoughts? _____

_____

9. Pragmatism

Do you consider yourself a more visionary or more pragmatic thinker, and why? _____

_____

10. Risk Taking

What are the biggest risks you have taken in recent years? Include ones that have worked out well and not so well. _____

_____

_____

11. Leading Edge

* a. How have you copied, created, or applied **best practices**? _____

_____

_____

b. Describe projects in which your **best practice solutions** did and did not fully address customer/client needs. _____

_____

_____

_____

c. How will references rate and describe your **technical expertise?** Are you truly leading-edge, or do you fall a bit short in some areas?

_____

_____

d. How **computer literate** are you? _____
_____

e. Please describe your professional **network**. _____
_____

12. Education

a. What **seminars** or formal **education** have you participated in (and when)? _____
_____

b. Describe your **reading habits** (books and articles—global factors, general business, function, industry). _____
_____

13. Experience

a. Compose a series of **open-ended questions**—"How would you rate yourself in _____, and what specifics can you cite?" For Sales Representatives, pin down the candidate's sales philosophy, actual style, familiarity with sales tools (such as lead tracking and reporting systems) and actual performance in relation to accountabilities (quotas, etc.).

• **Question:** _____ ? _____
_____

• **Question:** _____ ? _____
_____

• **Question:** _____ ? _____
_____

• **Question:** _____ ? _____
_____

• **Question:** _____ ? _____
_____

• **Question:** _____ ? _____
_____

b. What are the most important **lessons** you have learned in your career? (Get specifics with respect to when, where, what, etc.) _____
_____
_____

Personal Competencies

14. Integrity

* **a.** Describe a situation or two in which the pressures to **compromise your integrity** were the strongest you have ever felt. _____
_____
_____

b. What are a couple of the most **courageous actions** or unpopular stands you have ever taken? _____
_____
_____

c. When have you confronted **unethical behavior**—or chosen to not say anything, in order to not rock the boat? _____
_____
_____

d. Under what circumstances have you found it justifiable to **break a confidence**? _____
_____
_____

15. Resourcefulness

* **a.** What actions would you take in the **first weeks**, should you join our organization? _____
_____
_____

* **b.** What sorts of **obstacles** have you faced in your present/most recent job, and what did you do? (Look for passion and effectiveness in figuring out how to surmount barriers to success.) _____
_____
_____

c. What are examples of circumstances in which you were expected to do a certain thing and, on your own, went **beyond the call of duty**? _____

d. Who have been your major **career influences**, and why? _____

e. Are you better at **initiating** a lot of things or hammering out results for fewer things? (Get specifics.) _____

16. Organization/Planning

* a. How well **organized** are you? What do you do to be organized, and what, if anything, do you feel you ought to do to be better organized? _____

b. When was the last time **you missed a significant deadline**? _____

c. Describe a **complex challenge** you have had in coordinating a project. _____

d. Are you better at **juggling** a number of priorities or projects simultaneously or attacking few projects, one at a time? _____

e. Everyone **procrastinates** at times. What are the kinds of things that you procrastinate on? _____

f. How would you describe your **work habits**? _____

g. If I were to talk with **administrative assistants** you have had during the past several years, how would they describe your strengths and weak points with respect to personal organization, communications, attention to detail, and planning? _____

_____

h. Describe a situation that did **not go as well** as planned. What would you have done differently? _____

_____

17. Excellence

Have you significantly **raised the bar** for yourself or others? Explain how you did it—your approach, the problems encountered, and the outcomes. _____

_____

_____

18. Independence

a. Do you believe in asking for **forgiveness** rather than permission, or are you inclined to ensure your bosses are in full agreement before you act? _____

_____

b. How much **supervision** do you want or need? _____

_____

19. Stress Management

* a. What sort of **mood swings** do you experience—how high are the highs, how low are the lows, and why? _____

_____

_____

* b. What do you do when **stressed out**? (Look for exercise, quiet periods, etc.) _____

_____

_____

   c. Describe yourself in terms of **emotional control**; what sorts of things irritate you the most or get you down? _____

     _____

   d. How many times have you **lost your cool** in the past couple of months? (Get specifics.) _____

     _____

     _____

   e. Describe a situation in which you were the **most angry** you have been in years. _____

     _____

   f. Tell me about the most **frustrated or disappointed client/customer** you have had in recent years. _____

     _____

20. Self-Awareness

   * **a.** Have you gotten any sort of systematic or regular **feedback** (360-degree or otherwise) from direct reports, clients, peers, supervisors, etc., and if so, what did you learn? _____

     _____

   b. How much **feedback** do you like to get from people you report to, and in what form (written, face-to-face)? _____

     _____

   c. What are the **biggest mistakes** you've made in the past ten years, and what have you learned from them? _____

     _____

     _____

   d. What are your principal **developmental needs** and what are your plans to deal with them? _____

     _____

   e. What have been the most difficult **criticisms** for you to accept? ___

     _____

     _____

f. If you were to arrange confidential **reference calls with some of your major clients/customers**, what is your best guess as to what they would generally agree are your strengths and areas for improvement? _____
_____
_____
_____

21. Adaptability

* **a.** How have you **changed** during recent years? _____
_____

b. What sorts of **organizational changes** have you found easiest and most difficult to accept? _____
_____

c. When have you been so firm that people considered you **stubborn** or inflexible? _____
_____

22. First Impression

(Judge directly in interview.)

What sort of **first impression** do you think you make at different levels in an organization? _____
_____

Interpersonal Competencies

23. Likability

a. When were you so **frustrated** that you did not treat someone with respect? _____
_____

b. How would you describe your **sense of humor**? _____
_____

c. Tell me about a situation in which you were expected to work with a person you **disliked.** _____
_____

24. Persuasion

    a. Describe a situation in which you were **most effective selling** an idea or yourself. _____

_____

    b. Describe situations in which your **persuasion skills** proved ineffective. _____

_____

25. Assertiveness

    a. How would you describe your level of **assertiveness**? _____

_____

    b. When there is a **difference of opinion**, do you tend to confront people directly, confront them indirectly, or let the situation resolve itself? (Get specifics.) _____

_____

    c. Please give a couple of recent specific examples in which you were **highly assertive**, one in which the outcome was favorable, and one in which it wasn't. _____

_____

26. Communications—Oral

    *** a.** How would you rate yourself in **public speaking**? If we had a videotape of your most recent presentation, what would we see?

_____

_____

    b. Describe the last time you put your **foot in your mouth**. _____

_____

_____

    c. How do you **communicate** with your organization? _____

_____

27. Communications—Written

How would you describe your **writing style** and effectiveness in comparison with others'? _____

_____

28. Political Savvy

* **a.** Describe a couple of the most difficult, challenging, or frustrating company **political situations** you have faced. _____

_____

b. How aware are you of company **political forces** that may affect your performance? Please give a couple of examples of the most difficult political situations in which you have been involved, internally and with clients. _____

_____

29. Team Player

a. What will reference checks disclose to be the common perception among **peers** regarding how much of a **team player** you are (working cooperatively, building others' confidence and self-esteem)? ____

_____

_____

b. Describe the most **difficult person** with whom you have had to work. _____

_____

_____

c. When have you **stood up** to a boss? _____

_____

_____

d. Tell me about a situation in which you felt **others were wrong** and you were right. _____

_____

_____

30. Conflict Management

a. Describe a situation in which you actively **tore down walls** or barriers to teamwork. _____
_____
_____

b. Describe situations in which you prevented or **resolved conflicts**.
_____
_____

c. If two subordinates are **fighting**, what do you do? (Look for bringing them together now to resolve it.) _____
_____
_____

Motivational Competencies

31. Energy

* a. How many **hours per week** have you worked, on the average, during the past year? _____

b. What **motivates** you? _____
_____

32. Passion

a. How would you rate yourself (and why) in **enthusiasm** and charisma? _____
_____

b. Describe the **pace** at which you work—fast, slow, or moderate—and the circumstances under which it varies. _____
_____

33. Ambition

Who have been recent **career influences,** and why? _____
_____
_____

34. Compatibility of Needs

Is there anything we can do to help you if there is a job change (relocation, housing, etc.)? _____
_____
_____

35. Balance In Life

How satisfied are you with your **balance in life**—the balance among work, wellness, community involvement, professional associations, hobbies, etc.? _____
_____
_____

36. Tenacity

a. What are examples of the biggest **challenges** you have faced and overcome? _____
_____
_____

b. What will references say is your general level of **urgency**? _____
_____

Other Competencies

37. Question: _____ ? _____
_____

38. Question: _____ ? _____
_____

39. Question: _____ ? _____
_____

40. Question: _____ ? _____
_____

41. Question: _____ ? _____
_____

Summary

COMPETENCIES	MINIMUM ACCEPTABLE RATING	YOUR RATING	COMMENTS
Rating Scale: 6 = Excellent 5 = Very Good 4 = Good 3 = Only Fair 2 = Poor 1 = Very Poor			
1. Selling Skills			
a) Sales Approach			
b) Phone Selling Skills			
c) Active Listening			
d) E-mail Prospecting			
e) Closing Ability			
f) Objection Handling			
g) Cost Justifying			
h) Negotiating			
i) Retaining Customers			
j) Capitalizing on Marketing Programs			
k) Generating Referrals			
l) Leveraging Leads			
m) Capitalizing on Peak Selling Hours			
n) Managing Sales Support Resources			
2. Sales Knowledge			
a) Track Record			
b) Territory Knowledge			
c) Pricing Methods			
d) Margin Analysis			
e) Learning New Products			
f) Converting Strategy to Tactics			
g) Proposal Quality (ask for samples)			

	Rating Scale: 6 = Excellent 5 = Very Good 4 = Good 3 = Only Fair 2 = Poor 1 = Very Poor		
COMPETENCIES	MINIMUM ACCEPTABLE RATING	YOUR RATING	COMMENTS
Intellectual			
3. Intelligence			
4. Analysis Skills			
5. Judgment/Decision Making			
6. Conceptual Ability			
7. Creativity			
8. Strategic Skills			
9. Pragmatism			
10. Risk Taking			
11. Leading Edge			
12. Education			
13. Experience			
Personal			
14. Integrity			
15. Resourcefulness*			
16. Organization/Planning			
17. Excellence			
18. Independence			
19. Stress Management			
20. Self-Awareness			
21. Adaptability			
22. First Impression			
Interpersonal			
23. Likability			
24. Persuasion			
25. Assertiveness			
26. Communications–Oral			
27. Communications–Written			
28. Political Savvy			
29. Team Player			
30. Conflict Management			

*Resourcefulness is the most important competency. It involves passionately finding ways to get over, around, under, or through barriers. It is a combination of many intellectual, personal, motivational, management, and leadership competencies.

	Rating Scale: 6 = Excellent 5 = Very Good 4 = Good 3 = Only Fair 2 = Poor 1 = Very Poor		
COMPETENCIES	MINIMUM ACCEPTABLE RATING	YOUR RATING	COMMENTS
Motivational			
31. Energy			
32. Passion			
33. Ambition			
34. Compatibility of Needs			
35. Balance in Life			
36. Tenacity			
Other Competencies			
37.			
38.			
39.			
40.			
41.			

SMART & ASSOCIATES, INC.
37202 North Black Velvet Lane
Wadsworth, IL 60083
Phone: 847-244-5544 Fax: 847-263-1585
2007 © Smart & Associates, Inc.
www.SmartTopgrading.com

Appendix D

Reference Check Guide
for Sales Representatives

Applicant	
Interviewer	
Date	

2007 © Smart & Associates, Inc.

Reference Check Conducted by _____

Name of Applicant (A) _____

    Home Phone _____

    Office Phone _____

Individual Contacted _____

Title _____

    Company Name _____

General Principles

- In-depth reference checks should be conducted by the **hiring manager or one of the tandem Topgrading Interviewers.**
- Reference checks should be performed *after* the Topgrading Interview. Before conducting reference calls, ask the sales candidate for documentation of sales goals for the past five years, as well as W-2 forms for the past five years.
- Contact **all supervisors** in at least the past ten years.
- During the tandem Topgrading Interview, you ask the applicant the name, title, and location of every supervisor. After the interview, you (interviewers) decide which supervisors or others you would like to talk with, and ask the *candidate* to arrange those calls. High performers, A players, will get their bosses to talk and provide you with the phone number and the time when the person will be available to talk.
- Promise those contacted total **confidentiality,** and honor that promise.
- Create a tone in which you are a **trusted colleague,** a fellow professional who knows (A) very well, who just might hire (A), and who would be apt to better manage (A) if (reference) will be kind enough to share some insights.
- **Take notes,** and keep them six months.

Introductory Comments

Hello, (name of person contacted), thank you very much for accepting my call. As (A) indicated, we are considering hiring him/her and I would very much appreciate your comments on strengths, areas for improvement, career potentials, and how I might best manage him/her. Anything you tell me will be held in the strictest confidence. (Assuming concurrence . . .) Great, thank you very much. (A) and I have spent _____ hours together. I have thoroughly reviewed his/her career history, and I was particularly interested in his/her sales record when he/she reported to you. If you don't mind, why don't we start with a very general question.

Comprehensive Appraisal

What would you consider (A)'s:

Strengths, Assets, Things You Like and Respect About (A)?	Shortcomings, Weak Points, and Areas for Improvement?

Sales Accountabilities

Would you please clarify what (A)'s sales and other accountabilities were in that position? What was (A)'s actual performance in relation to those accountabilities? _____

_____

_____

Overall Performance Rating

On a scale of excellent, good, fair, or poor, how would you rate (A)'s overall performance? _____

_____

Why? _____

Reasons for leaving? _____

Would you rehire (A)? _____

Confirmation of Dates/Compensation

Just to clean up a couple of details:

What were (A)'s starting _____ and final _____ employment dates?

What were (A)'s initial _____ and final _____ compensation levels?

(Get base, bonus, and other compensation)

Description of Position Applied For

Let me tell you more about the job (A) is applying for. (Describe the job)

Good/Bad Fit

Now, how do you think (A) might fit in that job? (Probe for specifics)

Good Fit Indicators	Bad Fit Indicators

Comprehensive Ratings

Now that I've described the job that (A) is applying for and you've told me quite a bit about (A)'s strengths and weaker points, would you please rate (A) on eleven sales skills, six aspects of sales knowledge, and eight general competencies? An excellent, good, fair, and poor scale would be fine. Quick ratings on a 1-10 scale would be appreciated. (Include only the skills pertinent to your sales position.)

	RATING	COMMENTS
Sales Skills		
1. Phone Selling		
2. E-mail Prospecting		
3. Closing Ability		
4. Objection Handling		
5. Cost Justifying		
6. Negotiating		
7. Capitalizing on Marketing Programs		
8. Generating Referrals		
9. Leveraging Leads		
10. Capitalizing on Peak Hours		
11. Managing Sales Support Resources		
Sales Knowledge		
1. Knowledge of Your Industry		
2. Territory Knowledge		
3. Pricing Method		
4. Margin Analysis		
5. Learning New Products		
6. Converting Strategy to Tactics		
7. Proposal Quality		
General Competencies		
1. Thinking Skills: intelligence, judgment, decision making, creativity, strategic skills, pragmatism, risk taking, leading-edge perspective		
2. Communications: one-on-one, in meetings, speeches, and written communications		
3. Experience: education, sales track record		
4. Resourcefulness: passion to surmount obstacles, perseverance, independence, excellence standards, adaptability		
5. Stress Management: integrity, self-awareness, willingness to admit mistakes		
6. Work Habits: time management, organization/planning		
7. People Skills: first impression made, listening, the ability to win people's affection and respect, assertiveness, political savvy, willingness to take direction, negotiation, persuasion skills		
8. Motivation: drive, ambition, customer focus, enthusiasm, tenacity, balance in life		

Advice for Me as Hiring Manager

What would be your best advice to me as to how I could best manage (A)?

_____
_____
_____
_____

Final Comments

Have you any final comments or suggestions about (A)? _____
_____
_____
_____
_____

Thanks!

I would like to thank you very much for your insightful and useful comments and suggestions. Before we close, please let me know which of your comments I can share with others and which should be just between the two of us._____
_____
_____
_____
_____

SMART & ASSOCIATES, INC.
37202 North Black Velvet Lane
Wadsworth, IL 60083
Phone: 847-244-5544 Fax: 847-263-1585
2007 © Smart & Associates, Inc.
www.SmartTopgrading.com

Appendix E

How Topgrading Creates Corporate Wealth

Appendix E is the complete explanation of the net-present-value analysis of the cost of mis-hires, and of the calculated improvement in share price and market capitalization, both summarized in Chapter 2.

How to Save $96 Million in Costs of Mis-Hires

Let's analyze the net present value (NPV) of Topgrading as it relates to the costs of mis-hires in the sales department. Consider a 400 person sales force that is average in both annual turnover (40 percent) and mis-hire rate (40 percent). The total cost to the business over a five-year period is summarized in the following table:

FORTY-PERCENT MIS-HIRE RATE						
Year	1	2	3	4	5	Total
Total Sales People	400	400	400	400	400	
Annual Turnover Rate	40%	40%	40%	40%	40%	
Total Hires	160	160	160	160	160	800
Mis-Hire Percentage	40%	40%	40%	40%	40%	
Total Mis-Hires	64	64	64	64	64	320
Annual Cost ($K)	$36,064	$36,064	$36,064	$36,064	$36,064	$180,320
Discounted Annual Cost ($K)	$30,053	$25,044	$20,870	$17,392	$14,493	$107,853
Net Present Value ($K) $(107,853)						

With a $563K cost per mis-hire, hiring mistakes in the sales department over the next five years represent a $180M problem. Apply a 20-percent discount factor, which in CFO speak is also known as the cost of capital and is used to convert future dollars into present values, and the hiring woes will cost the company $108M, according to NPV calculations.

Let's assume that after reading this book, the CEO realizes the company is underperforming its peers in terms of hiring success and decides to deploy Topgrading according to the plan provided. The organization sets a conservative first-year goal of reducing its turnover and mis-hire rates from 40 percent to 20 percent. The following table charts the organization's progress:

TWENTY-PERCENT MIS-HIRE RATE						
Year	1	2	3	4	5	Total
Total Sales People	400	400	400	400	400	
Annual Turnover Rate	20%	20%	20%	20%	20%	
Total Hires	80	80	80	80	80	400
Mis-Hire Percentage	20%	20%	20%	20%	20%	
Total Mis-Hires	16	16	16	16	16	80
Annual Cost ($K)	$9,016	$9,016	$9,016	$9,016	$9,016	$45,080
Discounted Annual Cost ($K)	$7,513	$6,261	$5,218	$4,348	$3,623	$26,963
Net Present Value ($K) $(26,963)						

Over the same five-year period, with a $563K cost per mis-hire, the hiring problem is reduced by 75 percent from $180M to $45M in real dollars or $108M to $27M in today's dollars. In the first year alone, the company saves itself about $27M,

> In the first year alone, the company saves itself about $27M, yet the cost of rolling out Topgrading is only a very small fraction of this amount.

yet the cost of rolling out Topgrading is only a very small fraction of this amount.

Impressed with the early results from year one, the company decides to further embrace Topgrading in year two and sets the goal of achieving world class status by reducing its turnover and mis-hire rate to 10 percent. The impact on the mis-hire problem is summarized below:

TEN-PERCENT MIS-HIRE RATE						
Year	1	2	3	4	5	Total
Total Sales People	400	400	400	400	400	
Annual Turnover Rate	20%	10%	10%	10%	10%	
Total Hires	80	40	40	40	40	240
Mis-Hire Percentage	20%	10%	10%	10%	10%	
Total Mis-Hires	16	4	4	4	4	32
Annual Cost ($K)	$9,016	$2,254	$2,254	$2,254	$2,254	$18,032
Discounted Annual Cost ($K)	$7,513	$1,565	$1,565	$1,565	$1,565	$12,376
Net Present Value ($K) $(12,376)						

As you can see, the original $180M problem is reduced by 90 percent to $18M in real dollars, or from $108M to $12M in today's dollars. This tells us that Topgrading can reduce the 40 percent mis-hire problem to 20 percent in year one, followed by a reduction to 10 percent in years two through five. It also tells us that Topgrading can save the company $96M over five years, according to NPV calculations.

> Topgrading saves the company $96M over five years, according to NPV calculations.

How to Increase Your Market Cap $75 Million

At this point, we have shown that the total cost associated with mis-hiring sales people is staggering. But it would be doing the business case a disservice to stop here. Organizations and their leadership teams must answer to shareholders, who care only about share price appreciation. They do not value day-to-day cost-cutting measures that don't produce a return for them. So can Topgrading really generate the results shareholders are asking for? Let's just say that if you were impressed with the cost computations, you will be blown away by what follows.

Before we get started, a little setup is necessary. One of the most commonly used financial metrics to evaluate the value of stock is the price/earnings (P/E) ratio. It is a stock's price per share divided by its earnings per share.

The P/E ratio measures the value the market places on the stock relative to the wealth the company creates. For example, the P/E ratio of the technology sector, currently at 22, means that the average stock trading for $22 per share has a per share earnings of $1. Assuming the P/E ratio of a stock represents fair value and will remain constant, an increase in earnings per share will increase the price per share, and a reduction in earnings per share will cause the price per share to fall.

Market capitalization is calculated by multiplying the share price by the number of shares outstanding. A company with ten million shares outstanding and a $22 share price would have a $220M market cap. If the P/E ratio remains constant, increasing earnings 50 percent to $1.50 will drive share price up to $33 and will increase the company's market cap to $330M. The result from the increase in earnings is an additional $110M in shareholder wealth, or a 50 percent return on shareholder investment.

OK, enough setup. Let's look at a detailed case study to see how Topgrading and the sales talent lever of the SBI Formula for Sales Success drives mammoth shareholder value creation. Here are the base financial assumptions for a technology company with 400 sales people:*

------

* The source of the financial ratio data is the 541 companies in the information technology sector whose revenues are greater than $100M, based on 2006 financial performance according to Yahoo! Finance.

Income Statement	Amount ($)	% of Revenue
Revenue	$200M	100%
Cost of Revenue	$92M	46%
Operating Expenses	$94M	47%
SG&A	$70M	35%
Cost of Sales	$40M	20%
G&A Expense	$30M	15%
R&D	$24M	12%
Other Expenses	$4M	2%
Earnings	$10M	5%

Shares Outstanding	10,000,000
Share Price	$22
Earnings Per Share (EPS)	$1
P/E Ratio	22
Market Cap	$220M

Based on the mis-hire cost computations above, deploying Topgrading to reduce the mis-hire rate from 40 percent to 20 percent in the first year of the project reduces the size of the problem from $36M to $9M in year one. Of this $27M reduction, roughly $17M goes toward revenue growth and $10M toward gross Cost of Sales reductions. Accounting for increased costs associated with the additional revenue creation, the Cost of Sales as a percentage of revenue shrinks from 20 percent to 19.5 percent. Therefore, the year-one income statement looks like this:

Income Statement	Amount ($)	% of Revenue
Revenue	$216.8M	100%
Cost of Revenue	$99.7M	46%
Operating Expenses	$100.8M	46.5%
SG&A	$74.8M	34.5%
Cost of Sales	$42.3M	19.5%
G&A Expense	$32.5M	15%
R&D	$26M	12%
Other Expenses	$4.3M	2.0%
Earnings	$12M	5.5%

The company's profitability increases from 5 percent to 5.5 percent, a 10 percent improvement. With 10M shares outstanding, the new EPS is $1.20. Assuming the P/E multiple remains constant at 22, the new share price is $26.40, up from $22. The impact on the market cap is a staggering $44M increase, from $220M to $264M. That's right, $44M in shareholder value was created simply by leveraging Topgrading to improve the hiring practices of the organization in the first year of deployment!

> *That's right, $44M in shareholder value was created simply by leveraging Topgrading to improve the hiring practices of the organization in the first year of deployment!*

Blown away with the first year success of Topgrading, the leadership team decides this project will not suffer the fate of many other corporate initiatives and be phased out after the first few months. Instead, they further embrace Topgrading and set a more aggressive world class goal of less than 10 percent turnover and greater than 90 percent hiring success for year two.

Based on the mis-hire cost computations above, deploying Topgrading to reduce the mis-hire rate from 20 percent to 10 percent in the second year of deployment reduces the problem from $9M to $2M. Of this $7M reduction, roughly $4M goes toward revenue growth and $3M toward gross Cost of Sales reductions. Accounting for increased costs associated with the additional revenue creation, the Cost of Sales as a percentage of revenue shrinks from 19.5 percent to 18.8 percent. Therefore, the year two income statement looks like the following:

Income Statement	Amount ($)	% of Revenue
Revenue	$221M	100.0%
Cost of Revenue	$102M	46.0%
Operating Expenses	$101.6M	45.8%
SG&A	$74.6M	33.8%
Cost of Sales	$41.6M	18.8%
G&A Expense	$33M	15.0%
R&D	$27M	12.0%
Other Expenses	$4M	2.0%
Earnings	$13.4M	6.0%

The company's profitability increases from 5.5 percent to 6 percent, a 9 percent improvement. With 10M shares outstanding, the new EPS is $1.34. Assuming the P/E multiple remains constant at 22, the new share price is $29.50, up 12 percent from $26.40. The impact on the market cap is even more impressive, as it surges from $264M to $295M.

> *The impact on the market cap is even more impressive as it surges from $264M to $295M.*

Yes, another $31M in shareholder value was created in the second year of deployment simply by leveraging Topgrading to improve the hiring practices of the organization!

Name another opportunity your 400 person sales force would have to produce a 20-percent shareholder return while creating more than $44M in market cap value in the first 12 months of deployment, followed up by a 12-percent return and another $31M market cap increase during the second 12 months.

The results in this example are worth repeating. *Through the P/E leverage, Topgrading produces a 20-percent shareholder revenue increase, generating over $44M in shareholder wealth in the first year and a total of 34-percent shareholder return—16-percent compound annual growth rate (CAGR)—creating over $75M in shareholder wealth, in the first two years of deployment.*

Index

About the Authors

Brad Smart

Brad completed his doctorate in Industrial Psychology at Purdue University, entered consulting, and since the 1970s has been in private practice as President of Smart & Associates, Inc., based in the Chicago area. Brad is frequently acknowledged to be the world's foremost expert on hiring. He has conducted in-depth interviews with over 6,500 executives. He is the author of seven books and videos, including:

Topgrading: How Leading Companies Win by Hiring, Coaching, and Keeping the Best People (the world's best seller among 1,400 books on hiring since 1999),
The Smart Interviewer: Tools and Techniques for Hiring the Best,
Smart Parenting: How to Raise Happy, Can-Do Kids (with coauthor Dr. Kate Smart Mursau), and
Selection Interviewing: A Management Psychologist's Recommended Approach.

Brad has helped companies Topgrade by assessing and coaching teams, conducting Topgrading workshops, and providing books, handbooks, and videos to help clients Topgrade on their own. The resulting improvements in company performance have been featured on the cover of *The Wall Street Journal* and in many *Fortune* articles.

Partial List of Clients Served

American Heart Association
American Power Conversion

Bank of America
Barclays

Blue Cross Blue Shield
Cancer Treatment Centers of
    America
Dayton Power & Light
Dominick's Finer Foods
Easter Seals
EMC
Federal Government of Canada
Fifth Third Bank
General Electric
Hayes Lemmerz
HEB
Hillenbrand
Honeywell
Ingersoll-Dresser
Intelsat
JLL Partners
Johns Hopkins University

Kennametal
Lincoln Financial
MarineMax
Microsoft
Quaker Oats
RehabCare
Royal Bank of Canada
Shell Oil
Siemens
SPL WorldGroup
Travelers Express
UBS
Uniprise
Ventana Medical System
Vertrue
Wachovia
Wickes

Topgrading books, training videos, workshops, and the free monthly newsletter, *Topgrading Tips,* can be obtained at:

www.SmartTopgrading.com.
Contact Brad Smart at:
Brad.Smart@Topgrading.com,
847-244-5544.

Greg Alexander

Greg Alexander is the CEO of Sales Benchmark Index, a sales benchmarking and advisory firm that pioneered bringing the management discipline of benchmarking to the sales function. He works with CEOs across the globe, helping them to build world-class capabilities inside their sales functions. Sales Benchmark Index has built the largest sales benchmarking database in the world consisting of 10,900 companies, 260 sales metrics and best practices, across 19 industries with over 12 years of historical data. This database is leveraged across proprietary methodologies authored by Greg which allows organizations to understand their sales performance on a relative basis as compared to their peer group and world-class capability. Greg is the coauthor of *Making the Numbers: How to Use Sales Benchmarking to Drive Performance* (Portfolio, 2008), the first book published on the topic of sales benchmarking. Greg is frequently acknowledged as the world's foremost expert on benchmarking the sales function and was named *Sales and Marketing Management* magazine's "2004 Sales Manager of the Year" for his work at EMC Corporation. He is the President of the Atlanta chapter of Sales and Marketing Executives International, the world's largest association for sales and marketing executives, founded in 1935 with over 10,000 members. Sales Benchmarking books, reports, and tips can be obtained at: wwwsalesbenchmarkindex.com. Contact Greg at: greg .alexander@salesbenchmarkindex.com or at 888-556-7338.